A Deaccession Reader

Reprinted 2004

Cover: Frame courtesy of William Adair, Gold Leaf Studios, Washington, D.C.
        Photograph by Edward Owen.

Library of Congress Cataloguing-in-Publication Data

A deaccession reader / edited by Stephen E. Weil.
        p. cm.
    Includes index.
    ISBN 0-931201-50-0
    1. Museums--Collection management. 2. Museums--Acquisitions.
    I. Weil, Stephen E.
    AM133.D37 1997
    069' .5--dc21   97-43035
                                                                       CIP

A Deaccession Reader

Edited by Stephen E. Weil

Dedication

To the registrars of this country's museums, whose unswerving commitment to their collections has, in turn, earned them this volume's richly deserved dedication.

Table of Contents

Table of Contents

A View from Great Britain

A Case History from Canada

Statements of Professional Concern

Collections Management Disposal Policies

Appendix

Index

Introduction

by Stephen E. Weil

Good museum management in no way requires that every institution that can lawfully do so must establish a deaccessioning program. For some museums, such a program might be wholly inappropriate. For others, it might be premature. For still others, the periodic deaccessioning of a few collection objects might be in order, but the establishment of a full-fledged program would hardly be justifiable. On the other hand, good museum management does require that the governing authority of every museum that can lawfully do so must, at the very least, address the issue of deaccessioning and make a carefully considered decision as to whether the establishment of some regular means to cull its collection might not serve the museum's best interest. No museum can afford today to clog its scarce storage with unconsidered collections that have simply been allowed to accumulate and lie fallow.

By bringing together in one place a substantial number of the English-language texts concerning deaccessioning that have been published over the past two decades, this volume is intended to assist those who may be responsible for the establishment, design, or execution of a deaccessioning program. As will be readily apparent, these texts have appeared in a broad scatter of journals and other professional publications. In making them available in this format, AAM hopes to provide an important service not only to museum practitioners and those who sit on the governing boards that must ultimately resolve deaccessioning issues, but also to students in museum studies programs and interested members of the press and public.

Stephen E. Weil is senior scholar emeritus at the Center for Museum Studies, Smithsonian Institution, Washington, D.C.

That museum collections grow—and sometimes relentlessly—is simply a fact of life. Although such growth may occasionally be attributable to lax management, more often than not the reasons for it are perfectly valid ones. For museums that deal with aspects of contemporary life—whether art, history, science, technology, or communications—continuous collecting is a necessity if they are to maintain their contemporaneity. For natural history museums, it may be urgent to collect certain endangered material while it is still available. In museums of all disciplines, successor curators may have different tastes and interests than did their predecessors. New areas of collecting constantly emerge out of advancing technologies and changing patterns of public consumption. Private collectors, who must invariably die, are frequently motivated by tax or other considerations to bequeath all or parts of their sometimes highly desirable collections to museums. One way and another, museum collections grow.

How rapidly do they grow? Nobody knows for sure. In the data report from AAM's *1989 National Museum Survey*, the annual growth figures reported for the two preceding fiscal years were 4.3 percent and 5.4 percent respectively. Notwithstanding the survey's sophisticated statistical model, those figures seem remarkably high. At an annual compounded growth rate of 5 percent, for example, the size of collections (as well as the budget required to care for them) would double every 15 years. Employing a more conservative assumption, i.e., that the growth of museum collections is linear rather than exponential, at a 5-percent growth rate doubling would still occur every 20 years. By way of a reality check, consider that the aggregate collections of the Smithsonian Institution's various museums—with approximately 140 million objects, certainly the nation's largest holding—increased during a roughly comparable two-year period at annual rates of only .6 percent and .5 percent respectively.

Perhaps the most comprehensive effort made in recent years to chart the growth of museum collections was a study begun by the Smithsonian in the spring of 1975 that culminated in *A Report on the Management of Collections in the Museums of the Smithsonian Institution*, published in the fall of 1976. With respect to natural history collections—the Smithsonian's single largest component—the study found that the annual growth rate over the prior 10 years had averaged 1.8 percent. That figure was comfortably within the 1 percent to 2 percent growth rate that the Association of Systematics Collections had projected in 1973 for natural history museums generally. With respect to its other collections, curatorial estimates of their near-term growth (10 and 20 years out) were largely within a range of 1.5 percent to 5 percent. As the more recent figures from the Smithsonian indicate, those projections proved to be far too high.

What might well have accounted for this discrepancy is that the 1980s was the decade during which the museum community first began to focus more sharply on the costs associated with the care of collections. It was in 1983, for example, that wide circulation was given to the calculations of a Washington architect showing that it was then costing museums in the United States an average of $50 per year per object simply to heat, cool, clean, and guard the spaces in which they were being stored. One consequence of this new focus on the costs of collection care was a greater selectivity in making additions to collections. A second consequence was a greater willingness to consider deaccessioning not only as a means to refine collections through culling but, through the judicious use of deaccessioning proceeds, to upgrade them as well.

Although deaccessioning may be broadly accepted today within the museum community as an all-but-routine (which is not to say simple) aspect of collections management, to much of the public it still remains somehow at odds with what it conceives the museum to be: a permanent repository, a great barrel of amber in which things—once dropped—will be forever preserved. That the first section of this volume deals with the controversy touched off by the Metropolitan Museum of Art's highly publicized deaccessionings of 1972 is altogether fitting. In ways that can only be understood in hindsight, that controversy was a landmark event in the evolution of this country's museums. Prior to that time, the ways in which museums dealt with their collections was not a matter of any widespread concern, or even any particular public interest. The same can no longer be said. When a museum proposes today to deaccession one or more significant (or, sometimes, insignificant) objects from its collection, it is all but inevitable that a considerable degree of public discussion will follow.

The museum that intends to deaccession must be well prepared for that discussion. Few issues that museums face are as multidimensional. As this volume will suggest, generalizations rarely apply; virtually every proposed deaccession must be both examined on its own unique merits and considered from multiple perspectives. On the other hand, there is one generality with respect to deaccessioning that has clearly emerged since the early 1970s. And that is this: that deaccessioning questions can never be divorced from larger questions of collections management. Deaccessioning practices are inescapably intertwined with accessioning ones, and both must be framed within the larger structure of an institution's overall collections management policy.

In retrospect, it is startling how few written collections management policies were in place when the Metropolitan controversy erupted in the early 1970s. At the ALI-ABA annual course of study on "Legal Problems of Museum Administration"—for a quarter-century the leading venue for the discussion of preventive legal measures in museums—the formulation and implementation of such written policies was not even discussed until the course's 1979 offering in Fort Worth where Marie Malaro characterized such written policies as highly desirable, but not necessarily imperative. It was not until the early 1980s that the Smithsonian's various museums were required to have written collections management policies in place. And it was only in 1984 that AAM first made the adoption of a written collections management policy a prerequisite for a museum seeking accreditation or reaccreditation.

As those with actual experience in their preparation can testify, the formulation of a well-considered collections management policy involves far more than simply thinking through the procedures to be followed with respect to owned or borrowed collections. It also involves a thorough articulation of the museum's fundamental purpose and, above all, an analysis of the relationship of its owned collections to that purpose. That is the point at which the formulation of both accessioning and deaccessioning policies must begin. *What is it that this museum hopes or expects to accomplish? How do its owned collections relate to its ability to do so?*

Clearly, if the fundamental purpose of the museum is to preserve a particular collection—think, for example, of the Uffizi Gallery in Florence—then any question of deaccessioning answers itself. It is clearly inappropriate. On the other hand, if the fundamental purpose of the museum is an educational (or some other nonpreservative) one, then the question of deaccessioning may turn—at least in part—upon the relative utility of one or another object to the accomplishment of that purpose. Within the constraints of whatever deaccessioning policy a museum ultimately adopts, the question of utility is then one of the two basic inquiries with which the consideration of any specific object for deaccessioning must begin: *What utility does this particular object have in the museum's pursuit of its purpose? If it does not have any discernible (or, to apply a more stringent test, substantial) utility, is there any other compelling reason as to why it should be retained?*

The second basic inquiry is a legal one. *Under what conditions, if any, did this object come into the collection? Are there any restrictions that limit the museum's right to dispose of it in any manner it chooses? If so, what legal steps might the museum successfully take in order to have those restrictions removed or modified?*

If the responses to those threshold inquiries indicate (a) that there is no purpose-based reason why a particular object should remain in the museum's collection, and (b) that there is no legal impediment to its removal, then the remaining questions that follow largely concern such issues as timing, donor relations, public relations more generally, strategies for disposal, and the use of proceeds. Some museums of contemporary art, for example, make it a policy not to deaccession the works of still-living artists. Many museums in all disciplines avoid deaccessioning objects received as gifts from still-living donors without first obtaining the donor's approval. Some go still further and will seek to get approval from the spouses of deceased donors or even from heirs in the next generation. In others, there may be a self-imposed term of years following the receipt of a gift during which it will not be removed from the collection.

With respect to disposal, one issue that has remained unresolved after many years of discussion is whether a museum ought to try to maximize for itself any benefit to be realized, or whether it must make some effort (even to its own economic detriment) to place the material to be disposed of in another public institution or, even more specifically, in another public institution that serves its same geographic community. Although there are references to such an obligation in several professional codes of ethics (and, as well, in the collection management policies of a number of museums), one of the obstacles to its implementation has been the seemingly insuperable problem of determining the proper compensation for the acquiring museum to give to the disposing one.

In 1994, the New York State attorney general's office sought to address this problem by devising a novel set of rules to be applied in connection with the then-upcoming January 1995 auction sale at Sotheby's of some 800 deaccessioned paintings, paperweights, and other objects being disposed of by the New-York Historical Society. The ostensible objectives of these rules were (a) to determine a fair market price for the material to be auctioned, while (b) simultaneously giving New York State institutions an "inside" opportunity to acquire the material on better terms than might be available to private collectors or out-of-state institutions.

The attorney general's scheme was to work as follows: New York-based institutions—specifically museums, libraries, and archives—would be permitted to sit out the auction on the sidelines and then, following its conclusion, to step in and pre-empt any sales that had been made. This pre-emption was to be made at the hammer price recorded in the auction room less a discount that ranged downward from 10 percent in the case of the least expensive auction lots to 3 percent in the case of lots where the "successful" bid was both over $100,000 and exceeded the high pre-sale estimate. In addition to this price break, museums that made such pre-emptive purchases could apply for financing terms that would let them extend their payments over a five-year period. In exchange for these privileges, the acquiring museums would be required to keep the objects thus acquired in their collections for at least 10 years.

In actual fact, some 43 lots were pre-empted by New York institutions. Among these were the Metropolitan Museum of Art (which paid $2.2 million for a Florentine salver crafted in 1449 to celebrate the birth of Lorenzo de Medici; the presale estimate had been $3 million to $4 million), the Brooklyn Museum, the Corning Museum of Glass, the Museum of the City of New York, and nine other institutions.

Although several commentators said they thought more material would have been acquired for public collections if the discounts from the hammer price had been greater, their comments seemed to miss the crucial point. The truly important advantage given to the local museums was not the discount but the fact that they could stay on the sidelines and keep out of the bidding. What that in turn meant was that the prices realized in the salesroom could in no case have been higher—and in almost every case must have been lower, and sometimes substantially lower—than what they would have been if those same museums had been active competitors in the bidding process. One of the peculiarities of the system called English Auction—the bottom-up system employed in the United States for art auctions—is that it is the unsuccessful underbidder, and *not* the successful final bidder, who ultimately determines the hammer price. The hammer price will always be exactly one bid, generally about 5 percent, above the highest bid that the underbidder was prepared to make.

By eliminating any contest between the ultimate underbidders and the pre-empting museums—in essence, by disrupting the normal workings of the auction market—the scheme imposed by the attorney general all but guaranteed that local museums would be able to purchase those lots of interest to them for considerably lower prices than might otherwise have been the case in a genuinely open auction. Whatever benefit those museums reaped came, of course, directly out of the already shallow pockets of the New-York Historical Society. Was it really intended to tilt the outcome so greatly against the deaccessioning museum and in favor of the acquiring ones? Laudable as this New York experiment may have been in its intentions, it ought to be examined with extreme care before the museum community takes it for any kind of a precedent. If it is ultimately concluded that, in the disposition of deaccessioned material, institutional buyers *should* have preferential treatment over private ones, what would provide greater fairness to the deaccessioning museum would be a process in which the acquiring museums were required to participate in the auction in a normal fashion but were then entitled to a discount from the hammer price if and when they were the highest bidders.

No aspect of deaccessioning arouses stronger feelings today than the use of proceeds. Can a museum faced with the possibility of shutting its doors (or downsizing its staff, or curtailing its program) save its situation by selling off some of its collection and using the proceeds for operations? What is instructive is to follow the evolving treatment of this issue through AAM's successive codes of ethics. The 1925 code (AAM's first) briefly discusses a certain kind of deaccessioning (albeit somewhat different than culling)—"Museums should cooperate by exchange, sale, or otherwise so that a very rare object or specimen may be placed where it can best be studied and kept in association with closely related objects"—but does not seem to contemplate sales to private buyers or address the use of sales proceeds at all. Although the 1978 code treated deaccessioning at considerably greater length (including a reference to "disposal through the trade" as an acceptable means of disposition), it too is silent with respect to the use of proceeds. In sharp contrast, the code of ethics that AAM adopted in 1993 was nearly aborted during its gestation by a prolonged and furious controversy over a clause that, in its original version, would have restricted the use of deaccessioning proceeds solely to the replenishment of collections and, even in the form finally adopted, eased that limitation only so far as to allow museums of certain disciplines also to use such proceeds for "direct care of collections."

That the museum community can generally assent today to such a restriction is a sign of how greatly its understanding of deaccessioning and the issues surrounding it have grown over the past several decades. In looking through his own files on the topic, this author was astonished to disinter a text written in 1974 in which he and a coauthor had questioned whether the replenishment rule should be accepted as readily as it was then starting to be:

> To begin with, many of a museum's operating expenses relate directly to the custodianship of its collection: curatorial salaries and fringe benefits, storage, insurance, conservation, restoration, atmospheric controls, framing, photography, security, building and records maintenance, etc. The use of deaccession proceeds in these areas is for the benefit, and not to the detriment, of the collection. Beyond that, though, the connection between a museum's overall program and its collection is so complex that what may ultimately benefit the collection most will be expenditures made in such other areas as the museum's exhi-

bition or publications program. These can give the museum vitality and attract the donors and purchase funds through which the collection will ultimately grow further.

Over the years, the wealth of a museum tends to become concentrated in its collection. Unless some of that wealth is allowed to flow back into new programs, the museum may end with a first-class collection ill-cared for in a dilapidated (or even uninsurable) building by a second-class staff. The public interest might be better served by a more balanced approach.

Twenty-some years later the seeming logic of that can be recognized as a recipe for disaster. Should it ever become the accepted practice to cannibalize museum collections in order to raise funds for operating expenses, museums will face a dim future indeed. A structure of external support that has taken generations to build would be at risk. So too would be the public confidence without which no institution can long survive. So too would be that missionary zeal of staff and volunteers without which the museums of this country could not operate as they do today. If the deaccessioning process *does*, as some have argued, have a dark side, then it is this: that somewhere in the process the temptation may become irresistible to try to slide around the wise rules that the museum community has made for itself and, by one means or another, divert deaccession proceeds back into operations.

In the pages that follow, readers will find this and myriad other aspects of deaccessioning examined from a wide variety of viewpoints. For those about to enter the process (and, as well, for those who may be preparing themselves to resist it), the more deeply they can steep themselves in the arguments that have been made for and against deaccessioning, the more capably they ought be able to analyze, articulate, and advance their own positions. What they will discover along the way is that, fully addressed, deaccessioning questions ultimately involve some of the most profound aspects of a museum's existence—most particularly those that relate to its fundamental purpose. Regardless of their outcome, conversations that touch such depths can only be healthy for the museums they concern.

Deaccessioning Goes Public

By Donald Garfield

The disposal of objects from a museum's collection garnered major public attention in 1972 when reports of the Metropolitan Museum of Art's intention to sell some of its paintings hit the Sunday *New York Times*. The *Times*'s art critic John Canaday entitled his column "Very Quiet and Very Dangerous." Beginning with an allusion to unconfirmed reports that the Met was considering selling off canvases by the likes of Gauguin, Manet, Cézanne, Renoir, and Picasso, Canaday noted that such action was in line with American museum practice "now that cash is hard for them to find."

Not disputing the legality of such action if the works in question are unencumbered with restrictive language, he questioned whether the sale of museum objects is ethical and wise. The danger of short-sightedness is always present, he averred. Canaday also alluded to the political implications given that in 1969 the U.S. House of Representatives threatened to disallow the deduction of appreciated property for works donated to public institutions. Museums and others in the art world fought off this grave danger by arguing that donated objects were "for the public good" and in large part responsible for the blossoming of museums during the previous decades.

Canaday maintained that the revenue lost by allowing wealthy donors to deduct market value of works of art had to come from the public, which thereby could claim ownership of said works. "By any ethical standard, the public owns them. When such works are sold, the seller-museum violates a fiduciary trust, whatever the reasons for

Donald Garfield, former assistant director of publications for the American Association of Museums, is a free-lance writer specializing in arts and culture.

selling may be," he claimed. Deaccessioning, therefore, weakens the position of those supporting the public support of the arts through tax deductions.

As for the wisdom of deaccessioning, Canaday reasoned that if the works are minor they will fetch inconsequential proceeds on the market. Hence it is not worth the risk that what today is considered minor in later decades may assume great value with a change in attitude. For high-quality works, Canaday stated that their sale "must be the result of rationalization, blindness, or utter desperation." He refused to accept the argument that by deaccessioning a museum can achieve greater balance in its collection. "Selling from strength," he wrote, "simply means watering down." The *Times*'s critic viewed museums as "repositories of precious records," not "merchandise marts" or "esthetic stock exchanges." Moreover, works of art, he added, sold to the highest bidder, can be lost to the public forever. Finally, he asked, Is this matter of deaccessioning important? "As the only answer, not unless art is."

The Met's response came a week later (*The New York Times*, March 5, 1972) in a column written by its director, Thomas Hoving. "Very Inaccurate and Very Dangerous" began with a claim that Canaday's report on an impending Met sale was "99-percent inaccurate." Hoving countered the critic's charge of secrecy with assurance that when the board made a decision there would be a public announcement. He then offered the museum's track record in regard to deaccessioning, noting precedents for "public sales, exchanges, and disposal by private transactions." Indeed, he estimated that during the previous 20 years, 15,000 works of art had been deaccessioned. Rather than being cloaked in secrecy, the actions took place in full public view toward the ultimate objective, which was "to upgrade and refine the quality of the collections." Factors leading to deaccessioning never include esthetic reasoning but only whether works so considered are redundant or of lesser quality compared to others like them in the museum. Furthermore, Hoving noted, the name of the original donor is attached to the new acquisition and proceeds never go toward general operating expenses or building projects.

Hoving took issue with Canaday's depiction of a museum as a static repository, maintaining the Met is not a Library of Congress or an archive. The business of an art museum, he argued, is quality, and steps taken to further the overall excellence and balance of the collection conform to museum policy. He and his curators recognized "that connoisseurship means not only taking in, but weeding out." As for risks, Hoving stated that there were as great a number of risks associated with not buying as in selling objects from the collection. Nothing, he stated, "is more irrevocable than missing a great work of art."

Media attention to the sale of works of art by the Metropolitan continued into the fall of 1972. It led the Met's president, Douglas Dillon, to contribute a piece to *The New York Times* (Oct. 22, 1972), "The Metropolitan 'Sets the Record Straight.'" His goal was to describe the museum's disposal policy, referring to its venerable tradition with more than 50,000 works sold during the museum's history. Dillon repeated Hoving's characterization of the practice as being directed toward refinement and improvement of the collection, not subject to current esthetic fashion, respectful of donors whose gifts are deaccessioned, and exclusively applied to enabling new acquisitions.

Stating that no work of art that has legal restrictions has ever been sold, Dillon noted that in the light of the recent debate the board "reaffirmed and clarified its policy" that works of art valued over $10,000 require proof that the donor does not object to the sale. Donors were free to add legal restrictions if they so wished and many recognized the benefit of having their gifts in a collection that constantly enhances its quality.

To counter the impression that the Met's deaccessioning was capricious, the museum's president outlined the institution's deaccessioning procedures with its checks and balances. As for the means of disposal, Dillon responded to the suggestion that works be sold at public auction or directly to other museums. The objective is to "make the best arrangement possible for the Museum, whether by auction, exchange or direct sale." Finally, at a time when the Met's physical limits were known, Dillon argued that further growth should be in quality, not size of collection.

In *Report on Art Transactions, 1971-1973*, published the following summer (June 20, 1973) and circulated to the members of the museum, the Met inserted an explanation of its disposal procedures and the role of the state's attorney general. A special committee of the board of trustees recommended and the board adopted the following modifications to the existing policy:

The various steps currently in force, which provide numerous checks and balances including the approval of the Acquisitions Committee, will remain in effect except as modified.

The new procedures outlined below were developed after extensive discussions with trustees, members of the staff and representatives of the Attorney General of the State of New York who is statutory representative of the ultimate beneficiaries of gifts, grants, devises and bequests for educational and charitable purposes and of the public interest to which the Museum is devoted. The provisions for notice to the Attorney General in the following paragraphs as well as some of the provisions relating to restrictions or limitations on the use or disposition of works of art donated to the Museum were suggested by his representatives.

The provisions for notice are included to enable the Attorney General to be currently informed of proposed transactions. They are not intended to be a transfer of responsibility for management of the affairs of the Museum. The Attorney General recognizes that the primary responsibility for management of the Metropolitan has been and remains with its Board of Trustees.

The modifications of the disposal process may be summarized as follows:

1. The Museum will, as in the past, consistently honor legal restrictions attaching to the gift or bequest of any work of art. In addition, requests which do not impose any legal obligation accompanying the bequest or gift of any work of art will be respected to the extent feasible, unless modified by the donor or, if the donor is not living, the donor's heirs or legal representatives, on notice to the Attorney General of the State of New York.

2. No work of art valued by the Museum at $10,000 or more will be disposed of within 25 years following its receipt if objected to after appropriate notice, by the donor or the donor's heirs or legal representatives. This policy will apply to any work of art, including gifts or bequests which are not subject to any legal obligation or accompanied by any non-binding request.

3. No object, valued by the Museum at more than $25,000,

which has been on exhibition in the Museum within the preceding 10 years, will be disposed of until at least 45 days after the issue of a public notice identifying the work and giving the range of its estimated value based on outside appraisals. Copies of such notice will be available to museums, scholars and art historians who request them. At the conclusion of this 45-day period, public comments will be studied, and either the Board or its Executive Committee will again consider the work in question and make the final decision.

4. All future sales of works of art for cash valued by the Museum in excess of $5,000 will be at public auction, unless the proposed sale is to another museum or similar institution in which case consideration will be given to requests for extended times of payment.

5. Whenever it is proposed that the Museum offer for exchange or sale to another museum, or for exchange to any third party, an object valued by the Museum at more than $25,000, at least three disinterested outside appraisals will be obtained. In setting up the procedures for selecting such outside appraisers, the Museum will solicit the views of knowledgeable third parties.

6. The Museum's Annual Report will include a statement of the cash proceeds from the sale of objects disposed of during the relevant year, and will describe each object sold or exchanged valued at more than $25,000. All reattributions of major works of art made during the preceding year will also be discussed in the Annual Report.

7. Promptly after action by the Board of Trustees, the Executive Committee or the Acquisitions Committee to deaccession any work of art with a Museum valuation in excess of $5,000, notice will be given to the Attorney General of the State of New York at least 15 days (unless otherwise agreed upon with the Attorney General at the time) prior to the sale or exchange of such work of art, specifying the restrictions, if any, applicable to such work of art.

8. The Museum will continue to explore with other museums the possibility of joint purchases of works of art.

Report on Art Transactions, 1971-1973 opens with a section devoted to the museum's policy, history and procedure. Before reviewing previous instances of deaccessioning and outlining the step-by-step procedure for removing an object from the collection, the board stated the museum's policy as follows.

> The Trustees have three basic practices from which to choose, each of which has merit. They may continue to collect works of art by purchase or gift and sell or exchange nothing. This practice is followed by some national museums such as the Louvre but by few that are not government institutions. This approach affords complete protection against changes in artistic taste and the scholarly judgments of the experts. It preserves forever for the public whatever the museum may acquire.

> A second choice, which must be weighed, would permit sales or exchanges only with other museums or similar institutions operated for public benefit. This practice also has the advantage of keeping art under control of organizations operated for the public. It affords more flexibility than the first choice and on occasion may serve to strengthen the collections of the buyer and possibly both parties to an exchange. The Trustees would not wish to be bound to the limitations imposed by limiting sales or exchanges to other museums. Their primary duty is to the Metropolitan and its constituencies. The market for works of art is constantly in flux. Not all museums are in a position to make large cash purchases and some have little to exchange.

> A third choice, the one followed since the first disposals from the Museum in 1885, permits the Museum to sell and exchange works of art in order to refine and enhance the collections. This approach, passed on, reexamined critically and continued by succeeding generations of Trustees, is founded on the concept that the Museum's goal must be excellence as defined by the best scholarly advice it can obtain. What the Museum sells or exchanges and what it acquires is based on the judgment and recommendations of professional curators and scholars who spend their lives in the study, analysis, appreciation and evaluation of works of art.

> As shown in this *Report*, considerations relevant to a decision to sell or exchange a work of art include the following: whether the object is inferior, is a copy of another work, or has been erroneously attributed to an artist of historic importance; whether the object has been exhibited infrequently or not at all; whether the object has been requested for loans to other museums; whether it is by an artist well represented in the col-

lection by equal or better works; and whether the collection will be impaired by its disposal.

On Oct. 19, 1973, the state of New York convened a public hearing to discuss the matter of museums and their disposal policies. A group of museum professionals spoke before Louis J. Lefkowitz, attorney general of the state of New York, Julius Greenfield, assistant attorney general in charge of the Charitable Foundations Bureau, and Palmer Wald, assistant attorney general. The conference took place at Two World Trade Center in New York.

Lefkowitz's opening remarks expressed the attorney general's interest in the matter of deaccessioning:

> It is your [assembled museum professionals] responsibility—a responsibility I know you do not accept lightly—to take and guard and preserve the artistic and historic treasures entrusted to your care so that they may be available for all to study and enjoy.

> During the past year, events involving one museum and its practices in deaccessioning and disposing of works of art raised many questions in the public mind as to how well all museums were discharging their obligations as trustees for the public in their stewardship of works of art. One aspect of this trusteeship is, of course, to follow scrupulously any restrictions placed on the gift of a work of art.

> You are all, of course, charitable institutions, organized and operated as such under both state and federal law. To maintain your status, to have gifts made to you, for example, deductible in the income tax returns of the donors, to have your own income (on those rare occasions when you have any) exempt from taxation, you must follow certain rules and regulations governing your operations. But, it is not the fact of your exemption from taxation that gives my office a great measure of responsibility with respect to your activities. I do not mean 'second-guess'; I do not mean 'supervise'; I do not mean 'administer' or 'operate' or 'run.' I mean that my office has been given by law, long antedating the independence of our country, the high duty of representing the people for whose benefit you hold your charitable and educational assets and to ensure that their interest in those assets is not adversely affected. It is for this reason, and not because you are tax-exempt or because you may get

some small help from public funds, that my office is concerned with your activities.

Your health and prosperity are essential to the cultural health and prosperity of all our people. It is for that reason that I have asked you to share with me your views on a number of matters of great concern to all of you.

As you know, when the problems of the Metropolitan Museum of Art began to appear in the press, a number of items of legislation were proposed. . . . It was my opinion, at the time, that legislative action was premature. . . . On reflection over the passing months, it has seemed to me that the better approach to ensure the continued and, one hopes, renewed confidence of the public in our great museums, is through voluntary cooperation and self-regulation, and not through legislation at this time. I am afraid, however, that if some workable, voluntary system is not developed, tailored perhaps to various kinds of museums and to museums of differing sizes, legislation will again be introduced giving to the state greater control over the day-to-day operations of museums in the area of purchase and disposition.

It is not my purpose in suggesting this meeting to discuss matters of esthetic judgment. These are matters which I do not consider to be within my competence. This is true even though I deeply feel that the state should support cultural and educational activities of the kind that you represent. Nor do I suggest that the arrangement with the Metropolitan Museum of Art is necessarily or even logically one that should be applied to all museums. What I do suggest is that the museums must recognize that they are not private corporations, that they are answerable for their activities and that the public interest, which we all seek to serve, will be advanced by discussion of this nature.

Speakers addressed themselves to five questions the attorney general circulated to the participants:

1. To what extent should the disposition procedures agreed to by the Metropolitan Museum of Art be adopted by other museums?

2. How can museums increase cooperation with one another particularly in the area of joint purchase and exhibition of works of art?

3. How can the gift or sale of works of art from one museum to another be best facilitated?

4. What loan policy should be established to insure short-term and long-term loans of works of art from one museum to another?

5. Should legislation be proposed to prevent or control the export of works of art long associated with this country?

First to speak from the museum community was Thomas Nicholson, director of the American Museum of Natural History in New York and president of the New York State Association of Museums. Nicholson's remarks reflected the opinion of most subsequent speakers:

> We [Council of the New York State Association of Museums] don't wish to quarrel with the specifics of the procedures that were sent us by the Attorney General and the procedures another institution has chosen to adopt for reasons of its own. We really question the implications in the letter that such procedures as these are . . . should be accepted voluntarily by any given institution. Basically, I don't wish to argue with the merits or demerits of the procedures themselves. They are uniquely adapted to the problems of one institution. Each of us has its own problems and each has our own ways of trying to solve them. We know that we are regulated by a great many things, a body of laws. We are regulated by the circumstances of our own legal entity, the act of incorporation, the governance of the New York State Department of Education. We are regulated by our boards on most of which there are ex officio representatives of the very broad areas as well. We are regulated by our colleagues and of course by the public. Some of these regulations are more formal and some are less formal but, believe me, they are still there. So, I would question the premise that we are not adequately regulated. I say there is a body of law that does regulate our profession. There are ethics in our profession, some written and some unwritten, and of course there are controls in our institutions. And again in some institutions these controls are specific and written and in other institutions they are represented by a long body of tradition and by the specifics of control within the institution itself. . . .
>
> If I act unwisely, with respect to my policy concerning collections, believe me, my trustees will fire me and very quickly. If I act unethically, believe me, my colleagues in the museum profession will very soon isolate me and I'll get fired for that reason and perhaps if I go illegally there will be criminal and possibly civil proceedings brought against me. If I acted

suspiciously, I am confident that either *The New York Times* or the Attorney General's Office will very quickly see whether I violated any of the former.

The question is really should museums have a written policy with respect to these problem questions? I think most museums should struggle with the problem of developing a written policy. We have got problems of policy on many matters on which we were controlled by law and ethics as well that I am struggling with. Our problems are not only with respect to collections but also with respect to safety, security, purchasing, public affairs, publications, and the licensing of our resources to others, community relations, personnel problems, hiring problems, problems of labor relations, accounting, and bookkeeping. All of these matters I have to struggle with on a day-to-day basis. All of them concern my protection of the public interest one way or another and there are ethics that control me. . . .

What it comes down to is that each institution, each museum, really has to be self-controlling with respect to all of these matters, not simply the matter that the Attorney General brought to our attention. Each institution has to answer for itself whether its processes, its size, its complexity, the understanding within its staff, its relations to other institutions require it to have written guidelines on a given problem or whether the guidelines that have developed through tradition and relations to the profession are adequate.

Robert Buck, director of the Albright-Knox Gallery, commented: "Our museum has never felt the necessity of set procedures. . . . Our answer to this question [number one] is predicated by our desire to emphasize reserving the mobility and flexibility in governing collections and their growth which has resulted in the number of very fine collections consisting of various materials and exhibits throughout the state and the country. Certainly, it is hard to imagine that the procedures to which the Metropolitan has agreed would have much validity for museums other than art museums and further, that they would be helpful at all to smaller art museums such as the Albright-Knox at any specific point."

Stephen E. Weil, deputy director of the Whitney Museum of American Art in New York, added his voice to a chorus of museum professionals iterating Nicholson's basic point—that the regulations worked out between the Metropolitan and the attorney general do not generally apply to the vast majority of New York museums. Addressing the first question, Weil stated:

> We do not feel that the public interest would best be served if the procedures agreed to by the Metropolitan Museum of Art were extended to the Whitney or to other museums engaged with contemporary art.

> Our disagreement is not with the principle that today—regardless of what motives museums may have been founded with, whatever the past may have been—there is no argument today that museums can only continue to enjoy their privileges if they are operated in the public interest.

> We feel that these disposition procedures so ignore the realities of how museum collections have been assembled, how they can best be refined and upgraded, and how the art market actually works, that rather than furthering the public interest, we think it would damage it.

Should Hoving Be De-accessioned?

by John Rewald

Some 75 years ago, the learned, respected and suave Léonce Bénédite, director of the Luxembourg Museum for modern art in Paris, was highly embarrassed when the painter Caillebotte bequeathed 63 Impressionist pictures to his institution. Although admitting that he was violating the artist's will, Bénédite managed to accept only 38 works, less than two-thirds of the collection.

A few years later, in 1907, the same Bénédite rejected totally a gift of a dozen early murals by Cézanne. In 1952, the Louvre had to reach into a special fund to purchase just one of these.

French museums have no right to sell anything, but had Bénédite accepted these donations—distasteful as they were to him—and kept them in storage, some future colleague, as well as his countrymen, would have been delighted to rediscover those Cézannes plus the two Manets, eight Monets, 11 Pissarros and others from the Caillebotte bequest. Indeed, these would have added tremendously to the prestige of the new and special Musée de l'Impressionnisme, now installed in the Jeu de Paume.

The lingo that sounds so professional in the pronouncements of museum directors only serves to hide what they do not wish to spell out. Some of the words such as "upgrading," "duplication," "refinement," "quality," or "de-accessioning" were already fashionable in Bénédite's days. This gentlemen explained that "for lack of space,"

John Rewald was an authority on Impressionist and post-Impressionist art. He taught art history at the University of Chicago. "Should Hoving Be De-Accessioned?" was originally published in **ART IN AMERICA**, *Brant Publications, Inc., January 1973.*

he had excluded from the Caillebotte bequest only "work-studies" and "unfinished sketches." Among these, it should be mentioned, was Cézanne's large composition of *Bathers*, now in the Barnes Foundation, possibly the artist's "most finished" work. Bénédite also stated that Cézanne's murals were "not needed" because the painter was already represented in the museum through the Caillebotte legacy (from which he himself had deleted three pictures out of five).

Bénédite was not only learned, respected, suave and cynical, he was also blind. With that limited vision one is not allowed to drive a car, but one can, it would seem, direct a museum, although this may constitute an equal public hazard. The unfortunate thing is that nobody knows whether this blindness is shared by Thomas Hoving, Bénédite's worthy colleague who is director of the Metropolitan Museum. It may take some 30 to 50 years before the consequences of his dealings—a very appropriate word—can be judged. He may not be around then, nor will this writer, yet I can assure him that the arrogant Bénédite never dreamed that some day he would rank as villain while the name of Caillebotte would be written with letters of gold in the history of Impressionism.

It is of course impossible to doubt the integrity and good faith of Mr. Hoving's trustees, but his does not guarantee that they are immune to errors of judgment. As a trained art historian, Mr. Hoving must know that throughout the centuries artistic values have been subject to fluctuation. Ingres called Gothic cathedrals "barbaric." Is the staff of the Metropolitan less prone to mistakes, conditioned by the taste of the times, than Monsieur Ingres?

The most disturbing aspect of the Metropolitan's recent rash of sales is that they concern mostly modern French works, and neither Mr. Hoving nor Everett Fahy, his curator, both eminently knowledgeable in their own provinces, have any specific expertise in the field of European art of the last and present centuries. The Metropolitan has never had a specialist in this area and admitted as much when it asked Charles Sterling, curator of the Louvre, to prepare its catalogues of French paintings of the 19th and 20th centuries. Did Mr. Hoving consult Professor Sterling before de-accessioning works the latter knows intimately?

To provide at least some kind of check to the temptations to which museum directors are exposed when they need money and want to turn works of art into cash, the American Association of Art Museum Directors has recommended that no work should be sold without the approval of the head of the department involved. Though noble in principle, this is actually not enough since a museum's staff is rarely wholly independent of its director or trustees. As an added precaution, established scholars should also be asked for unbiased opinions.

Mr. Hoving and I happen to be in complete agreement on this point, since he proclaimed in the *New York Times* of March 5, 1972, that "every time" a de-accession is contemplated, the curator of the department concerned is "usually [?] asked to argue the case before his colleagues, the Vice Director and Curator-in-Chief, the Director and then the Acquisitions Committee of the Board. . . . In certain instances the advice of outside scholars is obtained." But does Mr. Hoving practice what he preaches?

Can Mr. Hoving produce the signed release for the secret sale of the large tropical Rousseau and van Gogh's *Olive Pickers*, recently revealed by the *New York Times*? I maintain that before disposing of such masterpieces, which lie outside the areas of specialization of the Metropolitan's staff, such authorities as Professor Meyer Schapiro, author of a book on van Gogh, and Professor Robert Goldwater, who has written on primitivism in modern art, should have been consulted.

But there are still other vices inherent to de-accessions. Some donations contain clauses that forbid any sales, and thus the decision to dispose of a specific work is not based *solely* on its merits or demerits but is accompanied by purely legal considerations. Certain weak pictures may belong to restricted legacies and cannot be gotten rid of, whereas better works may happen to be legally available for de-accession. This means that inferior objects can be safer from liquidation than much more desirable ones.

In addition there are also economic aspects to de-accessions. Pictures that are truly mediocre, such as those which the Metropolitan put into the Sotheby Parke Bernet sale of Oct. 25, 1972, or which were auctioned under the donor's name at Versailles last summer, do not bring much. Those which the Metropolitan sold or traded privately such as the van Gogh, the Douanier Rousseau, the Gris, the Modigliani (and who knows how many others), are good pictures and therefore worth considerable amounts. In other words, if one wants to raise cash through de-accessions, fine and desirable works provide more money than insignificant ones. When large sums are needed, only paintings of high quality will produce results (the word "upgrading" sounds strange in this connection). Therefore the museum finds itself in a grotesque position, totally contrary to the attitude of anyone who wants to *sell* something: Instead of boosting the work and saying how exceptional it is, the museum must appease its trustees and the press by declaring that it is a rather insignificant product, not good enough to grace its walls.

This peculiar circumstance may be one of the reasons why Mr. Hoving prefers to deal in secret with a foreign-based commercial gallery that doesn't mind acquiring "weak" modern pictures when they are masterpieces. Rather than acting openly or selling at public auctions, as the Guggenheim Museum does (whose massive de-accessions I nevertheless deplore), it would seem that the Metropolitan suddenly shuns all publicity. The tropical Rousseau, a recent bequest from Miss Adelaide de Groot, was deleted from a contemplated auction even before John Canaday sounded the alarm in the *New York Times* of Feb. 27, 1972. The sale, which was also to include the van Gogh and a "replacement" for the Rousseau (the latter a gift from the late Marshall Field), was subsequently called off. Those of us who had lined up against the Metropolitan's policy believed we had won a battle. How naïve we were. Mr. Hoving simply chose to proceed with his de-accessions in a different way. He has now learned, by the outcries of the press and the resolutions of various professional organizations, that he was suspiciously ill-advised—if he was advised at all—to negotiate exclusively with a *single* dealer.

But he did more: He misled us. Replying to Canaday's accusations concerning rumored de-accessions in a signed article of March 5, 1972, in the *New York Times*, Mr. Hoving solemnly asserted that "if and when the Board [of trustees] did come to a final decision, the Museum would make an announcement." A few weeks later he sold, obviously with the board's approval, the Rousseau and van Gogh paintings and made *no announcement* (to the contrary, he even tried to deny the secret deal when the press later confronted him with the facts). I herewith accuse Thomas Hoving of having broken a public pledge.

In a more recent letter to the *New York Times* (Nov. 1, 1972), Mr. Hoving listed, among prerequisites for successful disposal of works of art, "great knowledge, experience and intuition." His "knowledge" in the field of modern art is questioned here; his "experience" has been dealt with by John Canaday; as to his "intuition," it is an even less reliable instrument for vital decisions. Where was Mr. Hoving's "intuition" when he had Harlem on his mind and when he wrote the stupendously tactless foreword for that lamentable exhibition? (I used to read this foreword aloud in my seminars at the University of Chicago as a perfect example for students of what should *not* be done.)

It may well be that because he is not particularly attached to the French 19th century, Mr. Hoving finds it easy to dispense with outstanding works that, according to him, are of "no importance." Yet here lies a dangerous precedent. What if the next director of the Metropolitan were a specialist in Oriental art who, overriding the protests of his curators and upheld by his misguided trustees, felt no compunctions about raiding the Cloisters for unrestricted bequests or purchases? Continued over the years, each successive director could demolish departments that predecessors had knowingly and painstakingly built up. From "refinement" to "refinement," the Metropolitan would see its collections disrupted if not liquidated.

Mr. Hoving did of course consult his trustees, who represent the establishment elite of New York but who are *not* art experts. Among those who are themselves collectors, many rely on the advice of curators, consultants or dealers. And that is as it should be. Yet does this entitle the trustees to pass on the merits of a work to be de-accessioned? Making decisions for one's own collection does not carry the same responsibility as appraising the artistic qualities and values of a public trust, and possibly depriving future generations of irreplaceable treasures.

Some 20 years ago the Art Institute of Chicago "upgraded" its collection by acquiring a painting by Tintoretto and, in the process, deaccessioned numerous Impressionist pictures. The Tintoretto has now reluctantly been downgraded and carries the label: *Workshop of Tintoretto*. This means that its commercial value has declined to next to nothing, whereas that of the Impressionists which were traded for it has steadily risen.

The sins committed not only by the museum of Chicago, but also by those of Rhode Island, Minneapolis, Boston, the Frick Collection, and too many others, were sanctioned by their respective trustees. Are the trustees of the Metropolitan better qualified and less likely to err than those of other museums throughout this country, who let themselves be swayed by persuasive directors?

Collectors who cherish their possessions can, before they die, derive one last pleasure (and certain tax advantages) from them by leaving them for the enjoyment of the entire community. I am convinced that my friend, the late Dorothy Bernhard, did not bequeath the van Gogh she had selected for her home—but which was purchased through the Metropolitan with money she gave—either to Mr. Hoving, or his trustees, or even to the Metropolitan as an institution; she left it to the visitors of the museum who come there from all over the globe. Even though it may be legal to attribute the proceeds from the sale of her picture to the acquisition of a rare work by Carracci and name her among the donors, there is something vulgar about the thought that her name may henceforth be attached to a painting she never saw and for which she may not have cared.

This is exactly what Dorothy Bernhard's cousin, Mrs. Virginia Lewisohn Kahn, said in a letter to the *New York Times* earlier this year, when Mr. Hoving considered selling a fine Brittany landscape by Gauguin: "This happens to have been donated to the museum by my mother, Mrs. Sam A. Lewisohn, who intended to make it permanently available to the public. It was a painting she loved. It was *not her intention* [italics mine] to give the Metropolitan a negotiable security, so that some future curator could convert it into cash. . . ." Adelaide de Groot's cousin used the same words in a letter of protest to the same newspaper, specifying that it was the testator's *intention* that her pictures "should be held in trust for all the public to see." I am aware of course that the donor put no legal restriction on the gift.

Like his colleague Bénédite, Mr. Hoving does not shirk from trying to circumvent the spirit of a legacy, if he can get away with it. Is this the reward for donors who supported the Metropolitan? I find it impossible to believe that the trustees, leaders in many social spheres, are not always mindful of the intentions of donors. Do these decisions actually represent the trustees' thinking? If they do, how can we, the public, expect the slightest consideration?

Consideration is not a word used frequently in museum parlance, perhaps because it doesn't have two meanings. Some museum directors not only speak a special lingo, they also have double standards. When John Canaday erred identifying a portrait of George Moore by Manet that the Metropolitan intended to de-accession, Mr. Hoving promptly retorted that this was "not the glorious Havemeyer pastel vibrant with life and wit . . . but an unfinished painting. . . ." Indeed, it was, but this unfinished painting is just as "vibrant with life and wit" as the pastel. Moreover, to quote the Metropolitan's own catalogue, "it is especially interesting because it reveals [Manet's] method of working directly on the canvas in oil paint without preliminary drawing." The Metropolitan also has two other unfinished portraits by Manet, both of the singer J.-B. Faure, neither of which is "especially interesting" or "reveals" anything, and one of which has been cropped and considerably restored. Since they are not on exhibit, no interested visitor can tell whether they have been de-accessioned or whether they are held in storage because, as restricted gifts, they must be kept. The scholarly community has no way of knowing which works are available for study—even in storage—and which are not. The Metropolitan, a tax-exempt, educational institution, plays its cards extremely close to its chest.

Among the pictures that were "tentatively" part of the auction prepared last spring was a historic landscape by Cézanne, purchased directly at the Armory Show of 1913, the first work by the artist to enter an American museum. Though the Metropolitan's catalogue points out that this is "one of the very few that satisfied Cézanne sufficiently to lead him to sign his name. . . ." to it, Mr. Hoving was willing to sacrifice it, doubtless for what he calls the "refinement" of the collection. But the real refinement lay elsewhere. The picture was absolutely filthy, yet Theodore Rousseau, Jr., while curator, resisted all suggestions of cleaning it because, he said, it was painted too thinly. *After the picture was de-accessioned*, Mr. Fahy, in a desperate effort to "save" it, had the courage to have the grime removed and presented it once more to the board of trustees. In view of its regained splendor, it was *de*-de-accessioned and now hangs in the public galleries.

The most unbelievable thing in this case is Mr. Hoving's calm assurance, given to a *Newsweek* reporter, that "we take probably more time and care in disposing that we do in acquiring." If Mr. Hoving's time and care result in the rejection of a work he had never seen in proper condition and which had to be cleaned surreptitiously before its qualities were recognized and the de-accession order rescinded, then we must shudder for his acquisitions, to which he admits applying probably *less* time and care.

The Cézanne landscape now shows the artist's—not the Metropolitan's—unbelievable refinement. It even reveals the pencil lines with which the painter, unlike Manet, scrawled some preliminary indications on the bare canvas. And the freshness of its colors is such that, as a result of the cleaning, the generally suggested date of execution has to be changed. But Mr. Hoving is not concerned with "rewriting history" for Cézanne, he only does this for Greek vases.

Let it be said in passing that a cleaning of a similarly condemned Blue Period Picasso revealed new qualifies and details that led to its being removed from the de-accession list. As to a small canvas by the admittedly minor artist, Eva Gonzales, it was sold at auction in a shameful condition. When did Mr. Hoving examine it in a clean state?

The case of Miss de Groot's tropical Rousseau is somewhat different though by no means more savory. In 1947-48, Harry B. Wehle, then curator of paintings at the Metropolitan, devoted a short article to her collection in the museum's *Bulletin*. At the head of this article, in which only four modern works were reproduced, the Rousseau was illustrated and captioned "a characteristic view of an imaginary jungle." Mr. Wehle also stated that Miss de Groot's loan of such pictures "brought to the Museum's galleries *valuable* [italics mine] works by artists then considered germane to the Museum of Modern Art but not yet represented at the Metropolitan." The situation here was the opposite of the Caillebotte-Bénédite scandal; instead of refusing gifts that the Louvre later wanted badly, the Metropolitan first *wanted* these pictures but discovered 25 years later that it no longer had any use for them.

Rousseau's paintings pose many thorny problems; two catalogues of his works, by different authors, disagree on attributions and dates. (Not having been informed by the Metropolitan that the de Groot picture is actually "weak," one of the two authors was even impudent enough to reproduce it in color.) There is not a single person at the Metropolitan to whom anyone could turn with a question involving the authenticity of a painting by the Douanier. Yet the Metropolitan forces us to accept, without any possible appeal, its verdict concerning the quality of a major work by the artist. In the words of Robert Hughes of *Time*, the selling of the Rousseau was "an act of taste (Hoving's) arrogantly masquerading as historical necessity."

Mr. Hoving now declares that he was "satisfied" and even "happy" with the undisclosed price obtained for this painting. I, too, would be satisfied had I received what *looked* like a large amount for an object with whose artistic and commercial value I was not familiar. As Canaday has so pungently put it: "Mr. Hoving seems to be going into the picture-vending business with all the financial acumen of a small boy setting up his first lemonade stand."

Apparently relying on the "great manipulatory abilities" with which *New York* magazine once credited him, Mr. Hoving now asserts, concerning the Rousseau: "We couldn't have gotten a better price!" How does he know? He admits having dealt with only *one* buyer, and that one a dealer who, to my knowledge, does not subscribe to the ideals of the Salvation Army. Whereas Mr. Hoving maintains that the Rousseau was "of no importance to us" (which means of no importance to him and the other non-Rousseau connoisseurs at the Metropolitan), the buyer gloats about the picture he wants to resell: "In my opinion it's a masterwork." Although the buyer did not study art at Princeton, I'm afraid the truth is on his side.

As to the van Gogh canvas donated by Dorothy Bernhard, the Metropolitan's catalogue indicates that the artist did four versions of the gathering of the olives, adding: "It is difficult to say which is the painting known to have been made from nature, but the vigor and freshness of ours suggest that it was made on the spot." Mr. Hoving has done irreparable harm to students by depriving them of the study of such a significant work.

The obsessional elimination of "duplicates" is another lame excuse for de-accessioning. To the contrary, if the Metropolitan could obtain a second version of van Gogh's *Olive Pickers*, such as the one owned by Mrs. Enid A. Haupt, this would provide a unique opportunity to study the artist's approach to a subject when working from nature and when drawing his inspiration from one of his own paintings. Nothing could be more instructive. If the Guggenheim Museum could hang next to its so-called *Clockmaker* by Cézanne the other, quite different version, still in an American private collection, this would afford a glorious experience, almost like observing the artist at work. There are *no* duplicates among paintings, or drawings, or watercolors (or, strictly speaking, among hand-inked and hand-pulled prints), despite what all de-accessioners-in-chief of all of New York City's major museums may say. "A real master never repeats himself," says Dietrich von Bothmer, curator of Greek and Roman art at the Metropolitan.

Mr. Hoving graciously admits that "there will be mistakes in disposing, but they will not be as serious as mistakes in not getting." Are we really to believe that? When the Metropolitan recently acquired its admirable Velázquez, for which it apparently "did not have the expected price at hand," the underbidder was another prominent American museum that happened to have the amount available. In persisting in a senseless competition, the Metropolitan drove the price above an unheard-of $5.5 million. Had the Metropolitan let the picture go to the underbidder, it might have been knocked down for considerably less. Admittedly, this masterpiece would not have come to New York, but the Elgin marbles, the *Mona Lisa*, Giorgione's *Tempest*, Rembrandt's *Nightwatch*, Vermeer's *View of Delft*, Goya's two Majas, Cézanne's *Bathers*, van Gogh's *Potato Eaters*, Seurat's *Baignade* (and even Whistler's mother), to name only a few, are not on Fifth Avenue either, and never will be, because they belong to museums whose directors and trustees do not indulge in de-accessioning.

What really matters is that the Velázquez would still have come to the United States and been within comparatively easy reach. And the large Rousseau and the van Gogh might not have had to be deaccessioned to a "private collector" in Rome who let Frank Lloyd of the Marlborough Galleries sign the check and—mysteriously—put the pictures on the market at the Marlborough Gallery in London.

Unburdened by the Velázquez expenditure, Mr. Hoving might also have been able to purchase a Braque and a Matisse which, he says, the Metropolitan still lacks. This is a startling admission, because I had thought a hopeful contribution of some trustees was to acquire for themselves and later bequeath to their museum the works that the latter needs for a well-rounded representation. Has Mr. Hoving been so absorbed by de-accessioning and the gaudy face-lifting of the Metropolitan's plaza that he has had no time to impress his trustees with the desirability of adding good canvases by Braque and Matisse to their personal collections? Or are those which they may own now of such inferior quality that he already plans to de-accession them when they finally reach the museum?

Among the reasons frequently invoked for de-accessioning is lack of space. In terms of square feet the Douanier Rousseau and the van Gogh occupy *less than one-third* of the surface of Rosa Bonheur's highly expendable *Horse Fair*, a majestic exercise in futile dexterity. Together with Bastien-Lepage's kitschy *Joan of Arc*, Pierre Cot's titillating *Storm*, Bouguereau's insipid *Proposal*, and not one but two insufferable Gérômes, not to speak of a sugary Alfred Stevens and a stupid Gabriel Max (neither of which is listed in the museum's catalogue), this group of mostly blown-up period pieces represents more than 400 square feet, enough space for many new acquisitions.

But please do not de-accession them. Let them go back into storage from whence they were rescued by Mr. Rousseau in what Mr. Hoving may call his "elitist activities." The ever-growing number of visitors to the Metropolitan is now confronted with these dreary products that hang next to rare works by Ingres. Though Mr. Hoving pretends to be in favor of explanatory labels, no one has yet gotten around to informing unwitting viewers of the fact that Ingres and Rosa Bonheur do not belong in the same category (or the same room). Her painting and others like it should be preserved as evidence of the bad taste of a bygone era and of the cynicism of our days which treats them as though they were works of art. Let us not forget that museums, though repositories of the past, also reflect the preoccupations, ignorance, pretentions and false values of their own times.

On the other hand, we could easily make do without that dull *Forest in Winter* (55 square feet) by Théodore Rousseau, a fine painter when he restricts himself to modest sizes; the Metropolitan owns several of his small and exquisite landscapes. Mr. Hoving could also apply his compulsion for "upgrading" to Corot since the Metropolitan has quite a few—mostly indifferent—works by this master.

Strangely enough, three of the works formerly threatened by disposal or actually de-accessioned—Gauguin's Brittany landscape, Manet's sketch of George Moore, and Cézanne's picture from the Armory show—now hang in the galleries. Was this done to appease the early protesters in the hope that they would not find out about the secret deals? However, there are also some paintings missing, such as Gauguin's *Tahitian Girls with Red Flowers* from the William Church Osborn Collection, Cézanne's *Portrait of Boyer* as well as his *Rocks in the Forest*, both Havemeyer bequests, and the Douanier Rousseau's *Bièvre Near Bicêtre*, a gift from the late Marshall Field. In the present state of affairs, the visitor has the choice between supposing them in storage, at the restorer's, or away on loan; he may also fear that they have been secretly de-accessioned. Must we tremble henceforth for every masterpiece that is not on view?

Has it ever occurred to anybody at the Metropolitan that its high-handed practices can backfire and even hurt other museums? Francis Steegmuller has exclaimed publicly, "I wonder why any citizen should offer works of art to these arrogant institutions!" Immediately after the secret Rousseau/van Gogh deal became known, a former benefactor of the Metropolitan put a highly important, historic and magnificent Impressionist painting on the market instead of willing it to the museum. A fund raiser for at least one American museum has already been told by a prospective contributor: "Why come to me; if you need money, do what Hoving does and sell some of your pictures."

There are already too many precedents of this type. The Louvre lost valuable Impressionist pictures of the de Bellio Collection (a personal friend of the painters), a Vollard legacy (including some of the murals rejected by Bénédite), the Félix Fénéon Collection (from which it had to buy several small Seurats at auction), and the entire estate of Monet's son. Similarly, the Museum of Modern Art, for various reasons, did not obtain three important private collections: the Sam A. Lewisohn Collection (one of the few pictures he did leave to the museum was recently de-accessioned and traded, after which it was resold twice, both times at a considerable profit), the Stephen C. Clark and the Conger Goodyear Collections. The same thing can easily happen any day to the Metropolitan.

On the other hand, collectors throughout the United States will now realize that unrestricted bequests leave their donations—even when solicited—totally unprotected. Indeed, they would be well advised to specify that the beneficiary of their gift may only exchange it for a better work of the *same* school or artist, provided outside specialists and scholars are consulted. This would prevent a "duplication" Mondrian being traded, say, for a "fine and much-needed" Grandma Moses!

Mr. Hoving, appointed in April 1967, makes promises with the same ease with which he de-accessions masterpieces. He publicly stated that he would stay only until after the 1970 Centennial of the Metropolitan, since "all I can do will be done in five or six years." But now he has announced: "We plan to put on an exhibition in about a year and a half showing what we have gained as well as our failures." I suggest that in order to illustrate fully the credit and debit sides of his policy, he should also show all the de-accessioned works, including those whose disappearance may not as yet have been discovered. And to round out this display of his "manipulatory" astuteness, there should even be a list of the gifts the museum will not get, now that collectors know that their bequests are never safe from changes of taste, despite Mr. Hoving's declaration that no work of art is "disposed of because of esthetic reasons." Does he want us to understand that monetary considerations are the only decisive factors?

Finally, on Oct. 22, 1972, Mr. Douglas Dillon, president of the Metropolitan Museum, tried to set the record straight in the *New York Times* and affirmed many of the same things Mr. Hoving has repeatedly stated, though without explaining why what Mr. Hoving says is not always identical with what Mr. Hoving does. Nor has he clarified why, only two days earlier, the same newspaper wrote that the Metropolitan had felt the need for a new set of guidelines for its de-accessioning procedures shortly *after* the *Times* had disclosed that the museum had listed a number of works in its collection with various dealers for sealed bids. According to Mrs. Prudence Harper, head of the curatorial forum's executive committee, "last April the curators appointed a four-member committee to work out the detailed guidelines. The form was completed sometime during the summer and approved by the trustees and director some time after that." John Canaday's article having appeared on Feb. 27, the committee appointed in April apparently didn't consider the matter very urgent, especially since these guidelines had "been under discussion for almost five years."

Mrs. Harper specified that the new guidelines recommend that, before any de-accession, information be gathered as to "whether the work would be useful to another museum on loan. . . ." It so happened that among the many pictures sold last spring by sealed bids was one purchased by a dealer on behalf of another American museum! This clearly indicates that the guidelines *followed* the disposals, certainly another "manipulatory" achievement.

The president of the Metropolitan also failed to explain why, according to the same Mrs. Harper, the new guidelines stipulate "that the curator responsible for a particular work must signify his approval or disapproval of its disposition. His judgment, however, would *not be binding* [italics mine] on the director and trustees." This new system admittedly was completed "sometime during the summer." This proves that the new guidelines became *retroactive* to cover the secret sale of the van Gogh and the Rousseau.

Mr. Dillon went to great length to show how careful the Metropolitan is in its de-accessionings by insisting that "no work of art valued by the curator at $10,000 or over will be disposed of until it has been ascertained that there is no objection from the donor, or that there has been a reasonable inquiry among available heirs of the donor or testator. . . ." This sounds fair enough, but unfortunately, on Oct. 25, exactly three days after this declaration appeared, the Metropolitan hastily and at the last minute withdrew lot No. 11 from the Sotheby Parke Bernet sale that took place that very evening. This lot, catalogued as "Property of the Metropolitan Museum of Art" and reproduced in color, was deleted from the auction because of protests raised by the donor's widow. For another lot, permission to sell was urgently obtained from the sons of the donors exactly three hours before the public auction started. This painting was also reproduced in color and its disposal had been arranged with the Sotheby Parke Bernet Galleries for several months. Is this how the museum carefully *ascertains* that there are no objections before de-accessioning a work of art? Since I absolutely refuse to believe that Mr. Dillon would have knowingly misled the public, I must presume that he was never told of these shocking occurrences. It would obviously be a good idea for the Metropolitan to hire an expert who would coordinate its official words with its unofficial deeds.

We have come a long way—but made no progress—since the rumpus stated in February-March 1972. Mr. Hoving then answered an article in the *New York Times* with the indignant complaint that John Canaday had implied "strongly that the Metropolitan had been equivocal, clandestine and even possibly unethical. . . ." Those were Mr. Hoving's own words. In view of what has transpired in these intervening months there can be little doubt that what is happening at the Metropolitan appears *equivocal, clandestine and possibly unethical.*

The questions that remain to be answered now are: When will the Association of American Museum Directors follow the Art Dealers Association, the faculty and students of the City University of New York, the chairman of Yale's art department, and the director of the Smithsonian, by taking a stand on the policies of its member, Thomas P. F. Hoving, who so blatantly disregards not only the association's recommendations but also the principles set forth in his own statements?

When will Mr. Hoving resign?

Deaccessioning— The American Perspective

By Marie C. Malaro

P erhaps I should begin by pointing out that I have never been able to find the word "deaccession" in my dictionary. The fact that those who bless new words have never seen fit to recognize the term does not seem to bother many in the United States. We have been engaged in "deaccessioning" for years, and if there has been debate—and there has been—it has not been over terminology but over the practice which the term describes.[1]

First, let me define what I mean by deaccessioning: "It is the permanent removal of an object that was once accessioned into a museum collection." Accordingly, the term does not apply when an object is placed on loan by a museum (there is no permanent removal), nor does it apply if the object in question was never accessioned. For example, if a museum acquires an object but never accessions it because it is not deemed of collection quality, the disposal of that object is not a deaccession. There was never an intellectual judgment made that the object in question was worthy of indefinite preservation and, therefore, the removal of that object raises less formidable hurdles. Also, I use the term "deaccession" to cover the entire process of removal. In other words, for me, deaccessioning encompasses two major questions:

■ Should this object be removed?

Marie C. Malaro is an attorney and professor emeritus at George Washington University (GWU), Washington, D.C. For 11 years she was the director of GWU's graduate program in museum studies. "Deaccessioning—The American Perspective" originally appeared in Museum Management and Curatorship, *volume 10, 1991. It is reprinted with permission from Elsevier Science Ltd., Oxford, England.*

■ If so, what is the appropriate method of disposal?

I make this clarification merely because some limit the term to just the first issue—the decision to remove—and consider the method of disposal an administrative detail. From my experience it is more prudent to consider all aspects of a proposed removal before any decisions are made. Sometimes the method of disposal can raise more difficult questions than the issue of whether the object should go.

One more prefatory comment is in order. When discussing deaccessioning we must bear in mind both legal and ethical standards.

■ *Legal standard*—What I can and cannot do.

■ *Ethical standard*—What I should or should not do.

It is important to understand the difference because each standard serves a specific purpose, and when we confuse the two, intelligent discourse is all but impossible. The law sets the lower standard. It tells us how we must act if we want to avoid civil or criminal liability. We find the law in statutes or by reading decided cases—what the lawyer calls precedent. *The law is not designed to make us honorable—only bearable—* and therefore we often can engage in some highly questionable conduct and yet stay within the law. The law, however does have clout. If you are found guilty of violating the law you must pay fines or you may go to jail.

Ethics are a different matter. A code of ethics sets forth conduct deemed necessary by a profession to uphold the integrity of the profession. It sets a higher standard because it is based on principles of personal accountability and service to others. A code of ethics, however, frequently has no enforcement power. It is effective only if there is personal commitment and informed peer pressure. This distinction between law and ethics is very important to bear in mind when we look at the history of deaccessioning in the United States. We have very little law in the United States that inhibits deaccessioning, and we have a tremendous variety of museums that are governed mainly by independent boards composed of private citizens. Accordingly, we have had all sorts of museums experimenting with deaccessioning under a wide variety of circumstances. And we have everyone commenting on the ethics of each particular situation with little law defining what is actually enforceable. You name it, we have probably done it in the United States, so it is worthwhile to take a closer look at how we have fared.

Most museums in the United States are not controlled by the government. They are what we call nonprofit organizations—organizations incorporated to serve a public purpose but run by boards of private citizens. Support comes through private donations, grants, and some revenue-producing activities. It is estimated that well over 90 percent of the objects in United States museums have been donated. The nonprofit sector is deeply rooted in the American tradition, and one of the reasons we sustain this sector is to provide diversity. Anyone in the United States can start a museum for any purpose as long as the purpose falls within our broad definition of "service to the public." We have museums in this nonprofit sector of ever size and shape. For example, the Smithsonian Institution is not a government agency. It owes its existence to the bequest of an Englishman, James Smithson, who left his fortune to start, in the United States, an institution "for the increase and diffusion of knowledge." The Smithsonian is chartered as a nonprofit organization and is governed by an independent board of regents. The Metropolitan Museum in New York is an independently managed nonprofit organization, as are the majority of the almost 7,000 museums listed in our professional directory.

Under our laws a nonprofit organization has a broad range of powers, and one of them is the ability to dispose of its assets under the supervision of its governing board. Thus any museum organized as a nonprofit has an inherent right to deaccession material unless its charter specifically limits this right. It is possible for the creator of a museum to restrict the ability to remove objects as, for example, the Freer Gallery of Art in Washington or the Gardner Museum in Boston. Here under the terms of the donors' gifts no objects can be removed from those collections, but these instructions reflect the wishes of private parties, they do not reflect public policy. What all this means is that whether a museum in the United States engages in deaccessioning is pretty much left to its governing board, acting in light of its own particular circumstances.

Added to this is the factor that the United States, with very limited exception, has never seen fit to restrict the movement of cultural objects located within its borders.[2] In fact, cultural objects can leave the country more freely than they can enter. What we have then is no centralized policy regarding collecting our collections and a government that plays no discernible role in shaping a national cultural policy. What is collected and what is disposed of is usually left in the hands of those who are interested in a particular museum. But all is not *laissez-faire*. Perhaps to fill a void, the museum profession in the United States talks a lot about ethics and public accountability. Several of our major professional organizations promulgate codes of ethics and each code has something to say about deaccessioning. The codes recognize deaccessioning as a valid practice, but set down guidelines for implementation. For example, the code promulgated by the American Association of Museums makes the following points:

1. Every museum should have a public statement regarding its policy on deaccessioning.

2. When considering disposal, the museum must weigh carefully the interests of the public that it serves.

3. When disposing of an object due consideration should be given to the museum community in general as well as the wishes and financial needs of the institution itself.

4. While the governing board bears the ultimate responsibility for a deaccession decision, great weight should be given to the recommendation of the curatorial staff regarding the pertinence of the object to the mission of the museum.[3]

The code promulgated by the Association of Art Museum Directors stresses the following points:

1. Deaccessioning should be related to policy not to the exigencies of the moment.

2. Procedures for deaccessioning should be at least as rigorous as for the purchase of major works of art.

3. While final decisions rest with the governing board of the museum, full justification for a disposal should be provided by the director and the responsible curator.

4. Funds obtained through disposal must be used to replenish the collection.[4]

A careful reading of each code shows that both professional organizations require a museum to have a policy regarding deaccessioning, both place final decision-making responsibility with the governing board (as the case law in the United States requires) and both require that the board pay attention to curatorial opinion, but in other respects there are different emphases. The Association of Art Museum Directors addresses the use of proceeds from deaccessions and insists that these proceeds be used to replenish the collections. The American Association of Museums, which represents all types of museums, has (at the time of writing) nothing in its code about use of proceeds from deaccessions. Instead, it speaks of considering the needs of the museum community generally when one is contemplating deaccessioning. In other words, there is less focus on dollar return, with more emphasis on trying to place the unwanted object with another collecting organization. These differences in the codes of ethics themselves highlight the fact that even in a country where deaccessioning is generally accepted there are differing views on its implementation, and differences frequently can be associated with discipline. For example, art museums are quite comfortable with sales in the marketplace but there is great pressure to require that sale proceeds be used only to replenish the collections. History museums seemed more concerned with finding an appropriate new home for a piece, and less stress is put on the matter of what is done with any proceeds that may accrue. Anthropology museums and natural science museums tend to favor only exchanges with other collecting organizations. These differences can be explained in part by the fact that up until recently only art brought substantial prices in the marketplace. With this factor changing, because now there seems to be a market for almost anything, and with the very high sale prices we have seen over the last few years, history museums as well as natural science museums are being forced to grapple with the lure of the marketplace.

If I were listing recent developments in the United States that are affecting deaccessioning this might be the first one:

Development 1. The very active and lucrative market for not only art but other collectibles has put added pressure not only on art museums but on all types of museums.

There are other developments that have been equally if not more responsible for renewed attention to deaccessioning. One is the fact that in 1986 a new tax reform act was passed in the United States, which makes it less attractive at times for individuals to donate objects to museum collections. As I mentioned earlier, museums in the United States depend almost exclusively on donations to form their collections. With donations down this means that collections will not grow unless museums can buy in the marketplace—buy, in many cases, the very works that would-be donors are now selling. But where is the money to come from, especially with prices escalating? A logical solution for many is to look for objects to deaccession and sell in order to raise purchase money.

The second development then is:

Development 2. The change in the United States tax law that discourages donations of objects to museums and forces museums to consider buying.

But there have been more profound and pervasive developments. Over the last decade or so the museum community in the United States has begun to examine itself more carefully, and this has been brought about by several factors. One is that there is more public interest in museums. As people become more educated and more affluent they are demanding more from museums and they are questioning the quality of governance in museums. At the same time we are seeing more professionally trained people attracted to museum work. In an effort to respond to the greater demands on museums these people are examining in a comprehensive way how their museums operate. Too often what they find are: disorganized collections, poor documentation, and horrendous storage conditions. A natural response is to re-examine the collecting practices of a museum so that there is some assurance the museum will collect wisely and that objects, once acquired, can be maintained, conserved, and used effectively. Accordingly we have a growing number of museums in the United States that have refocused their collecting activity and are seriously concerned about proper maintenance and conservation of their collections. Because of this, I can add to my list two other developments that are affecting deaccession activity. These are developments not usually highlighted by the press when a deaccession story makes the newspapers, but they are of fundamental importance.

Development 3. Many museums have more carefully focused their collecting and now find themselves with objects that are extraneous to their missions.

Development 4. Because of heightened concern for quality storage and conservation, museums are questioning the validity of retaining objects that are not clearly furthering the goals of their museums.

Because of all the above-described developments we are seeing more deaccessioning activity in the United States and, as might be expected, renewed debate concerning the practice. Most of the newspaper stories and magazine articles feature major art museum deaccessions because these are always more dramatic and often involve the disposal of a work or works in order to acquire immediately a preferred replacement. This allows everyone the opportunity to play critic on the merits of the particular exchange and some, in their zeal, call for the outlawing of all deaccessioning. I do not believe it likely that the United States in the foreseeable future will consider seriously any legislation that would ban deaccessioning. Such a move would be at odds with our concept of a museum and with our whole tradition of leaving cultural development in the hands of the people rather than the government.

On the first point—our concept of a museum—we view museums essentially as educational organizations with responsibilities to collect wisely, maintain prudently and encourage public use and enjoyment. Collecting in an educational organization is not a mechanical process. It is a combination of intelligent selection and periodic re-evaluation. What serious educator would ever take the position that what is deemed "right" today should never be subject to review? But this attitude is inherent in a general prohibition against deaccessioning. How can a museum present itself as an educational organization and yet relinquish a continuing responsibility to review critically its progress in achieving its particular goals? Accordingly, in the United States, the prevailing view is that if museums want to be considered educational organizations they must be free to deaccession.

The second reason for arguing that the United States would never seriously consider outlawing deaccessioning is our tradition of leaving cultural development in the hands of the people—as evidenced by our nonprofit sector. This system, which encourages great diversity, has served us rather well. We have museums that never dispose of anything, others that are free-wheeling, and every shade in between. Each can survive as long as enough people are willing to support it. By encouraging diversity we encourage the direct participation of many in shaping a cultural heritage. A ban on deaccessioning, which would seriously inhibit the present system, just does not make sense.

While I would argue that the last thing the United States needs or wants is any legislation inhibiting deaccessioning, I will readily admit that our museum community is not without fault in this area. The weak spot is not the general rules we have developed for deaccessioning, it is a failure to promulgate these rules as aggressively as we should. If more time and effort were to be spent educating the profession with regard to these general rules, the few problems we have with deaccessioning would probably disappear.

Our general rules are all drawn from our major codes of ethics, and they reflect our very American view that each museum is responsible for its own destiny. Our rules give wide discretion to those in authority within a museum, but they also require that those in authority answer directly to the people they serve and on whom they depend for support. The general rules on deaccessioning are essentially these:

1. Deaccessioning should never be addressed in isolation. It is dependent on a clear articulation of a museum's collecting goals and prudent acquisition procedures. In other words, deaccessioning is not a method for curing sloppiness in accessioning. A first consideration, therefore, is to have strict acquisition guidelines in place.

2. Collections should be reviewed periodically for relevance, condition and quality. When this is done routinely more objective opinions result, and with no urgency to remove, there is time to reflect on initial judgments.

3. There should be written policies and procedures on deaccessioning. These should stress thoughtful review, clear delegation

of responsibility, careful record-keeping and public disclosure. The policies and procedures should address:

a. reasons that may justify removal;

b. the importance of clarifying the museum's unrestricted title to an object before it is considered for removal;

c. the role of professional staff in the process;

d. when outside opinions are to be sought;

e. appropriate methods of disposal that may be considered;

f. who has final responsibility for deciding whether an object is to be removed;

g. who has final responsibility for deciding the method of disposal;

h. who is responsible for keeping records of the process;

i. who is responsible for providing information to the public on a planned disposal;

j. when and how notification of deaccessioning is given to donors of objects;

k. the importance of avoiding even apparent conflicts of interest in the deaccessioning process.

A museum that has such written policies and procedures—and follows them carefully when deaccession situations arise—will probably make sound decisions and will maintain public confidence. This is so because in the very process of preparing its deaccession policies and procedures the museum will have re-examined its mission, clarified its collecting goals and pondered the long-term effects of its actions. Also, it will be acutely aware that the burden of justifying deaccessioning decisions rests with it. After all this preparation, the museum is truly ready to take on individual cases, and as decisions are made the museum will be able to convey a sense of purpose and thoughtful adherence to previously articulated goals. This is the essence of good governance.

However, I must mention that I am always rather perplexed by the amount of controversy we see on the subject of deaccessioning as compared with the general apathy concerning the issues of mindless collecting or collecting with negligible documentation. Is the public better served by an undisciplined or poorly documented collection? I would suggest that if there is persistent agonizing over deaccessioning the museum profession should look more deeply. Those who cannot come to terms with deaccessioning may be avoiding taking decisions in other areas of collections management. When you look at the total collection management picture within a museum, and demand that all facets be reviewed and controlled in light of the museum's mission, the matter of deaccessioning falls into perspective. It becomes a small part of an integrated plan and, as such, it can be handled with confidence and in a way that inspires confidence.

In conclusion, if there are lessons to be learned from studying deaccessioning in the United States they are these:

a. In order to justify deaccessioning you must first be able to demonstrate that the museum has control over its collections. Control means that there is a collecting plan which is in accord with the mission of the museum, and the plan is religiously followed.

b. You must be able to demonstrate that your collections are periodically and objectively reviewed for adherence to collecting goals.

c. You must have written procedures for considering proposed deaccessions, and these procedures should stress full discussion, clear delegation of decision-making authority and complete record-keeping.

If these lessons are followed one does not have to worry about deaccessioning being used as a quick and shallow solution to immediate problems. By the time a museum has taken all the required steps and is at a point where deaccessioning can be considered it will have educated itself. What decisions are then made should be relatively thoughtful, supported by clearly articulated policies. This approach offers the public the greatest protection because it demands that the museum profession understand and practice the full scope of its responsibilities.

END NOTE (MAY 1991)

In May 1991, the American Association of Museums adopted a new code of ethics [revised 1994]. The new code requires each museum, as a condition of membership, to adopt its own code of ethics that applies the association's code to its institutional setting. The purpose of this provision is to strengthen self-regulation through self-education. The new association code adds yet another element to its deaccessioning guidelines. The new element, which echoes an earlier provision in the code of the Association of Art Museum Directors, reads:

"[U]se of proceeds from the sale of collection materials are restricted to the acquisition of collections."

Notes

1. Some claim the word merely demonstrates ignorance of Latin. *Ad cedere* is the Latin for "to cede to" or "accession." *Decedere* is the Latin for "to cede from" or, logically, "decession." Somehow we "deaccession" or "cede from to."

2. The exceptions are mainly archaeological objects removed from federal or Indian lands. Federal statutes control the use of these objects. States may have similar statutes regarding such materials found on state property.

3. *Museum Ethics* (American Association of Museums, 1978).

4. *Professional Practices in Art Museums* (Association of Art Museum Directors, 1981).

Selling Items from Museum Collections

By Steven H. Miller

M useums exist because of an assumption that physical objects have value. Museums therefore collect, care for and explain all manner of human artefacts and naturally created objects. Their collections are believed to have inherent importance. When acquiring an item a museum is saying that for one reason or another the item is worthy of being preserved by and for the general citizenry. In the United States most museums, though private, operate as public trusts directly and indirectly supported by the taxpayer. That such a system survives and seems to flourish indicates a certain acceptance that it is desirable and works. Central to this scheme is an overall notion that assigns precedence first and foremost to the physical well-being of museum collections.

People visit museums with different expectations and for many reasons. One thing they all assume (if they think about it) is that what they see there was acquired and is being preserved, for them, in perpetuity. Directly, and by inference, they have been repeatedly told this. One can find little museum literature that does not regularly discuss this primary task. Until recently people had no reason for disbelief. But lately people have learned that on occasion museums sometimes remove things from their collections. This practice, which has come to be called "deaccessioning," is now beginning to be recognized as part and parcel of a museum's

Steven H. Miller is executive director of The Bennington Museum, Bennington, Vt. "Selling items from Museum Collections" originally appeared in Museum Management and Curatorship, *volume 4, 1985. It is reprinted with permission from Elsevier Science Ltd., Oxford, England.*

operational choices. This was not always so. Though weeding out from collections may be as old as museums themselves, only recently was the practice accorded formal recognition by the museum profession and given a name. This development is probably good, and a mechanism should exist that allows museums to remove items responsibly. Things enter museum collections for many reasons, not all of which are grounded in a well-meaning desire for patrimonic preservation or aesthetic enlightenment. Some items enter museums solely for reasons of personal aggrandizement, others to gain tax benefits. Some are accepted as favors, others because of a momentary lack of good judgment. A few seem to sneak in when no one is looking, and thus not all may be appropriate. Deaccessioning, however, must not be taken lightly, and its purpose and ramifications must be carefully studied and understood if it is to be effective.

The fact that museums subtract from as well as add to their collections received widespread public attention in the United States in 1973. A series of scathing articles written by John Canaday, art critic for the *New York Times*, exposed a scheme adopted by the Metropolitan Museum of Art in New York which involved the selling of art works from their permanent collections. Most of these were paintings given by Adelaide Milton de Groote. These articles, and the rebuttals and discussions that followed, created quite a stir. The issue became one of such acrimony as to attract the attention of the New York State attorney general as well as to be described by some as a major museological scandal. Certainly the matter was of more than fleeting local concern. For the first time those inside and outside museums were made aware of a practice that in may ways seemed diametrically opposed to what museums stood for. The effects of the publicity and the attendant debate are still being sorted out.

In the past decade museums and museum organizations acknowledged the need for deaccessioning by drawing up various policy guidelines on the subject. These were usually brief. Often they were put together in the frenzy of the moment out of genuine concern for a dilemma within the profession previously unaddressed, and to satisfy possible inquiries. In many cases a standard form was adopted, with a few adjustments made to meet the philosophical needs or practical concerns of the individual museum. Fortunately this situation is beginning to change as deaccessioning continues to be scrutinized. The process that results in the decision to deaccession can be convoluted or simple. It depends on the nature of the museum, the personalities and experiences of those responsible, and the circumstances of the moment. Museums put forward many reasons for wishing to remove items. Among the easiest to understand are: The museum ceases to exist; it can not properly care for an item; it changes purpose; it does not legally own the item; the item is not germane (e.g., it should not have been there in the first place, or, research has altered its scholarly status); or the item poses a physical danger to people or property. Some of the more nebulous reasons given for deaccessioning include: the need for money, a lack of visitor or research interest in an item, changing tastes, the refinement of the collection or the item is considered to be a duplicate.

Key questions that surround deaccessioning are: what, why and how? The last may be considered the easiest to answer but when the options are examined in light of what museums are supposed to do, caution is advised. Nevertheless, the "how" of deaccessioning may have more profound effects than the "why." Usually a number of avenues are open. An item can be destroyed, given to a private or public party, traded or sold. Whichever method is chosen, allowing something to become privately owned again may in the long run have devastating consequences, on both the individual item and museums in general. Selling presents an especially onerous set of problems. A simple, often open, and remunerative method of disposal, it can raise issues that cut to the quick of the *raison d'être* of museums. When deaccessioning was brought to public attention in the 1970s and museums addressed the matter by drawing up policies, the hope was to avoid future allegations of wrongdoing. There was (and is) a very real desire to be transparently honest, open and above board if a time should come when something was to be removed from collections. The concept of full public disclosure, as an insurance against allegations of "insider trading," was warmly embraced. The commercial sector seemed to satisfy these requirements as well as offering the bonus of the money which was always needed. The auction houses and the galleries were seen as a highly visible, neutral and democratic forum for deaccessioning. But such commercial activity can rankle with people. By allowing for the possibility of something in the public domain becoming privately owned, it subjects that item to a loss of its intellectual or historical pedigree, and assigns to it a monetary value. Also it can subject an item to grave physical dangers.

People get testy when what they perceive to be public property is made available for private ownership. Recent citizen outrage over the way the United States Department of the Interior was managing national wilderness and park properties is a perfect example. Secretary James Watt's policies implied to the general public an abrogation of duty and reneging on a promise. So too with museums when they sell from their collections. An implied price tag is suddenly attached to everything a museum owns, and such deaccessioning can spread a cloud of mistrust over all acquisition and collection management practices. Interest in the commercial deaccessioning of museum collections is growing, and depending which side of the fence one is on, the arguments offer apologies for, defensively rationalize, vehemently oppose or applaud the practice. A recent example can be found in the April 1984 issue of *ARTnews*. An article about the sale of original architectural drawings owned by the Frank Lloyd Wright Foundation clearly addressed the problem.

Officials . . . defend the sale, saying the money is needed to maintain the archives and refurbish. . . . They consider it a success, claiming that, with several of the works still unsold, the show has already brought in almost $2 million. Many museum officials and architectural historians, however, consider it a failure—of faith. They think breaking up the archives is an outrage; the foundation's responsibility is to keep the collection, which includes all but a few hundred of Wright's drawings, together.

. . . the sale was done through a gallery . . . That type of sale gives the best buying opportunity to individuals, who can decide to spend money quickly. Museums and public institutions take too much time to raise funds. Indeed, although several of the private owners may eventually donate their work to public collection _____ and _____ named only one buyer who almost certainly purchased a drawing for a museum.

The result is not only that the archives are being dispersed but that they are being dispersed into private hands.[1]

Another illustration which vividly points out the pros and cons of commercial deaccessioning occurred recently in New York City. The Museums at Stony Brook, N.Y., which is famous for its holdings of the 19th-century artist, William Sidney Mount (who lived in the museum's region), wished to improve that collection. They wanted a painting which in their opinion was of superior quality. The painting was for sale at an unaffordable price, so to raise the money the museum sold at auction two of its paintings by the same artist. In so doing a record price was set for the artist's work. The substantial profits realized by the sale enabled the museum to purchase the painting they wanted. Of the two paintings sold, one was bought by a museum, and the other is now in private hands.

The fashion that grew in earnest in the 1960s for collecting virtually everything has resulted in skyrocketing prices for a great variety of art and antiques. This robust new market can exert strange pressures on museums. The astronomical prices obtained are noted, and when the profit realized from the sale of one painting could more than equal an annual budget, buy a new building, increase staff or pay for new acquisitions, the temptation to look and see what might be disposed of is strong. As moths are drawn to candle flames so are some museums lured into the commercial maelstrom. The marketplace is naturally ecstatic about increased museum deaccessioning activities. It is not unusual these days for museum personnel to be approached by art and antique dealers with offers to trade, buy or act as sales agents for commercially desirable items in museum collections. One of the most telling indications of the rush to get a piece of the deaccessioning action is seen at the leading auction houses. Sotheby's and Christie's have both established museum services departments, and these organizations are falling all over themselves to attract what they perceive as a potentially lucrative segment of a new market. Fancy invitations, champagne receptions and press parties are just some elements of the razzle-dazzle that accompanies deaccessioned museum items when led to the unknown fate of the auction block.

Museum audiences deal with economics every day. The influence of money on how they live, work, think and act is profound. But there are many aspects of their lives in which money plays a minor role. Usually these have to do with certain intellectual experiences, personal feelings and social habits, one of which is visiting museums. Visitors may have visions of great riches when they enter grand marble halls hung with examples of the world's finest art, or when they view golden objects from ancient cultures. In the long run, however, it is the social, educational and intangible aspects of museum visiting that people enjoy most. To interrupt that flow of ideas by interpolating thoughts of price-tags and impermanence disrupts a unique experience. Except for the matter of affordability, monetary value should have little to do with why museums acquire or dispose of objects. The old saying "the buck stops here" can be easily applied to an item when it enters a museum. Only for insurance purposes do collections have pecuniary value, and their importance lies in their historic, scientific and/or aesthetic qualities alone. In selling items from their collections, museums reverse this position. They are perceived to be saying that the price of the item supersedes its scholarly, educational or spiritual value. If something is good enough to sell, is it not good enough to save?

There are practical considerations that warn against deaccessioning by selling, not least that it may influence adversely potential offers of gifts to museums. In previous years the idea that a donated item might someday be disposed of was rarely given a thought, so secure was the trust of donors; but today it is common to discuss the possibility, occasionally with most unfortunate results. When the Mark Rothko Foundation recently divided up its share of the estate of this foremost abstract expressionist painter, one of the prime reasons stated for giving the bulk of it to the National Gallery in Washington, D.C., was that the institution in question has a policy of not deaccessioning.

From the point of view of the physical conservation of collections, a matter allegedly of primary concern to museums, commercial deaccessioning as currently practiced in the United States makes little sense. The vicissitudes of the art and antique market are not friendly to the physical well-being of its stock-in-trade. Auction houses, individual dealers and private galleries have an unfortunate record of breakages and thefts. In the course of being bought and sold items are subjected to traumatic environmental changes, and when damage occurs, a quick, inexpensive cosmetic repair is the order of the day rather than proper conservation attention. Most items sold return to private ownership and are then subjected to further grave risks. Poor storage, hazardous display conditions and incompetent handling regularly wreak havoc. The problem is further aggravated in that few owners possess any knowledge about conservation or have access to responsible advisors on the matter.

In addition to the practical and intellectual problems created by commercial deaccessioning, the act can further be seen as violating the simple rules of common courtesy. Such fears may seem silly but museums owe their very existence to social mores and the subtleties of human interactions. Usually items enter museum collections because someone wanted them there. Reasons for this vary, but they tend to center around a desire to contribute to the well-being of society and to be remembered posthumously. The giving and receiving of an item, or the money to purchase it, is an act of faith in and by a museum. When accepting such offers a museum is establishing a relationship which it should be bound to honor. Deaccessioning can be seen as a repudiation of this agreement. It raises questions about why the item was accepted in the first place, why it is being removed by sale, and the fate that ultimately awaits other acquisitions. The answers, whether real or imagined, can cause people to reconsider their support of museums. More than most human endeavors, museums survive on goodwill, and to do everything possible to maintain that goodwill would certainly seem logical. The personal wishes and feelings of those who made, and make, acquisitions feasible must not be given short shrift, though this does not necessarily mean acquiescence to every whim or demand of a donor.

Real or perceived disrespect in matters of collection care and disposal can seriously erode the hard-won confidence which is crucial to every museum's existence, especially in the United States.

One factor contributing to commercial deaccessioning (and perhaps not yet fully recognized) is growing out of a desire to be seen as fiscally responsible and managerially competent. These laudable goals are causing a flurry of activity within the museum field which focuses upon learning the way and the jargon of the corporate world. Getting an M.B.A. is no longer anathema to museum workers. There is almost a trend developing that sees the adoption of business practices as possibly a magic elixir to cure all museum ills. Managing museums by the standards and practices of the corporate sector has had varying degrees of success. It has been applied to a range of operations, including those concerned with collections. One frightening result is that museum acquisitions are occasionally looked upon as "assets" in much the same way a firm might see its office furniture, land, buildings, equipment, etc. This is most glaringly expressed in those museum annual reports which "capitalize" collections, listing total values as a stock inventory (a practice that mercifully seems to be in decline). Considering collections as business assets establishes a working premise in which concern for their well-being can become unreasonably subservient to the greater fiscal health of the museum. The rise of the museum in public estimation has caused those responsible to become extremely sensitive about how items from collections are disposed of, and no one wants to be accused of giving the stock away. What once might have been passed on to another museum is now more likely to be sold. It is human nature to balk at relinquishing an asset in a way which might be construed as foolish or not in one's best interests. To be sure, museums are not immune to financial realities, and if they are to survive they must be solvent, but is it wise in pursuing this goal to allow collections to be cannibalized?

Another problem posed by deaccessioning, especially by sale, has to do with the matter of public record. When an item enters a museum collection that act becomes a recorded public fact. In addition to whatever spiritual and social roles museums may fulfill they also undertake very practical ones. Daily they are called upon by scholars, researchers, the general public and others who require information of all sorts. Most seek to examine objects in the collections, and to have to say "No, that item was sold and we don't know where it is" seems to be a contradiction of that function.

Lurking behind deaccession decisions are always legal considerations. These can range from the simple, such as those involving straightforward proof of ownership, to more complicated problems involving intertwined interests of donors, rights of artists, museum obligations, etc. The most obvious legal matters are usually examined closely by responsible museums considering deaccessioning. But whatever is done and however it is accomplished, very strong cases against certain ways of deaccessioning, especially commercial public sales, may be easy for critics to make. Questions stemming from the tax deductibility of an item might be taken into account, and it would not be surprising if, in the United States, the Internal Revenue Service began to look suspiciously on a practice that made it possible for tax deductions to be realized on an item more than once. (Of course, to follow this line of inquiry to its logical conclusion would mean that once an item had been used for a tax deduction it would lose all future deductibility—an intriguing concept to say the least.) However, there are times when deaccessioning by sale may very well be the best or only route available to a museum. Perhaps no other preservation institution is interested in having the item no longer required, or legal requirements oblige sale. Occasionally such purely utilitarian objects as office furniture have come to be accessioned, but by and large there are usually viable alternatives to commercial deaccessioning which give the future well-being of the deaccessioned object first priority.

Items removed from museums could be offered to other museums either by sale, trade or gift. Such an idea could be agreed in principle by museums on an *ad hoc* basis, or within a more organized formal structure. The availability of such items to be deaccessioned could be made known in a number of ways. Notices could be published in museum professional literature, or an organization could be established which would oversee the relocating of deaccessioned items. A kind of worldwide collections clearing house, it would be dedicated to keeping items in the public sector and to assuring their future physical, aesthetic and intellectual integrity.

The past two decades have witnessed dramatic changes in museums and the role which they play in different societies. They have been placed in the centre ring of the cultural circus. Rare today is the city that does not proudly boast at least one museum, and in accepting the new attention directed towards them, museums must take care. Their success is having direct and profound effects on all aspects of their being—most especially on their collections. These are receiving unprecedented attention, and depending on one's point of view collections are: intrinsically of interest, the bait used to attract notice for other purposes or the camouflage behind which is sought social or academic prestige and acceptability. The growing public profile of museums has resulted in heightened competition, and the need to keep museums afloat and prosperous, as well as make those responsible for them look good, has intensified. Collections have not escaped these new conditions. The better the collections the more highly respected the museum, and new acquisitions are the spiritual manna that prove an institution's worth. Therefore, all holdings are being subjected to a new intensity of scrutiny. At best this results in long overdue and much-needed scholarly attention, enhanced public appreciation and improved conservation. At worst it is reducing collections to merely convenient vehicles for social aggrandizement—not exactly a secure environment for either their physical longevity or scholarly integrity.

Museums are the only inventions of humanity to be devoted solely to preserving our artefacts. Museums today tend to enjoy a high level of credibility, and their popularity is stronger than ever. But this new-found pedestal can be a curse or a blessing. It demands vigilance in all things, and especially in the treatment of collections. Public perceptions of museums must be carefully tended; if not the results can be devastating. Deaccessioning rests on a clear understanding of an individual museum's capabilities, policies and goals, but it also has to do with what museums in general are attempting to achieve. There is a triple responsibility that any museum must always bear in mind. It is directed to the institution, to its collections and to the public. If the best interests of all three are served by removing an item from a museum, without endangering the item itself, then deaccessioning is probably being carried out correctly. However, when commercial considerations reign supreme, the process is grossly polluted.

Notes

1. Michael Kimmelman, "The Frank Lloyd Wright Estate Controversy," *ARTnews*, 83, no. 4, April 1984, pp. 102-105.

Deaccessioning in American Museums: I

By Stephen E. Weil

In a typically acerbic annotation to *The Works of Sir Joshua Reynolds*, William Blake observed, "To Generalize is to be an Idiot. To Particularize is the Alone Distinction of Merit."

Blake's observation holds true for museums. Generalizations about museums most often miss the mark. The general question of how a museum ought best manage its collection—no less the more critical inquiry as to what sort of policy it should adopt with respect to deaccessioning—cannot begin to be addressed without reference to the particular kind of a museum that it is. While virtually every museum is, to a degree, engaged in the three core functions of preservation, study and public communication, the relative emphasis that it gives to each of those functions may vary markedly from one institution to another.

For the museum that is chiefly depository or archival—one that takes its principal mission to be the preservation of specimens and artefacts that might otherwise be lost to posterity—the issue of deaccessioning will scarcely arise. If to preserve more examples of something is simply considered more worthwhile than to preserve fewer, then the very notion of refining its collection must *per se* be antithetical to such a museum's basic vision of its mandate. That would hold true as well for any museum initially established not for some living purpose but to serve as a static memorial or shrine.

Stephen E. Weil is senior scholar emeritus at the Center for Museum Studies, Smithsonian Institution, Washington, D.C. "Deaccessioning in American Museums: I" first appeared in the August 1989 issue of APOLLO *magazine. Reproduced courtesy of* APOLLO *magazine.*

Deaccessioning might be equally inappropriate for the museum that makes scholarship its primary goal. The fact that an object may no longer be suitable for public display might be irrelevant in terms of its potential for research. Likewise, the fact that an object might be duplicative or otherwise redundant would not necessarily diminish its utility: Similar objects might, for example, be usefully subjected to dissimilar forms of investigation.

For the museum that is fundamentally devoted to public communication, however—and in the United States, at least, that would include most museums of modern and contemporary art—the situation is different. The collection of such a museum is neither intended principally to be an end in itself nor to serve primarily as a subject for research. The collection of such a museum has been gathered and is maintained for the purpose of public education. Periodically to shape and reshape such a collection in order that it may better serve the museum's purpose—to rid the collection of objects which, although relatively useless to its needs, continue to drain the museum of the resources required for their care—may be more than merely permissible or appropriate. In such a museum, the process of shaping and reshaping its collection, of pruning and winnowing to the end that the collection may be upgraded and supplemented, might well be the hallmark of a sound, dynamic and farsighted approach to collections management.

More and more, American art museums are deaccessioning what they consider to be superfluous or redundant works of art. This can be clearly seen by examining the catalogues of the major auction houses. Last autumn's sales in New York, for example, included paintings and sculpture consigned to auction by the Art Institute of Chicago, the Baltimore Museum of Art, the Sterling and Francine Clark Art Institute and the Hirshhorn Museum and Sculpture Garden. Other recent auctions have included works of art consigned by, among others, the Museum of Modern Art, the St. Louis Art Museum, the Metropolitan Museum of Art, the Phillips Collection, the Whitney Museum of American Art and the Los Angeles County Museum of Art.

That American art museums may today feel less hesitant than formerly with respect to such deaccessioning should not, however, suggest that such a practice has developed wholly without constraints or that it can be pursued willy-nilly. On the contrary, a number of rules, some formal, others less so, have accumulated around this practice. Perhaps the most important of these is that a museum must use the proceeds from deaccessioning to benefit its collection. This is specifically laid down in paragraph 27 of *Professional Practices in Art Museums*, the guide to ethics and standards first promulgated by the Association of Art Museum Directors (AAMD) in 1971. This provides that:

> The deaccession and disposal of a work of art from a museum's collection requires particularly rigorous examination. Deaccessioning should be related to policy rather than to the exigencies of the moment, and funds obtained through disposal must be used to replenish the collection.

In several recent instances, institutions that proposed to use the sales proceeds from deaccessioned objects for other purposes have been persuaded to change their plans in whole or in part, when the AAMD took the position that to do so would constitute a "breach of principle." This was the case when Harvard proposed, late in 1981, to deaccession works of art from its Fogg Art Museum in order to raise operating funds for what was to be a new wing for the museum. Faced with a formal statement of condemnation, Harvard initially cancelled the new wing entirely. When this produced an even greater storm of protest, the university found other means to construct and maintain the new wing.

A more recent instance involved the Phillips Collection in Washington, D.C. In 1987, the Phillips announced that it had deaccessioned and planned to sell *Le Violon*, a 1914 Cubist painting by Georges Braque, a work which Marcel Duchamp had personally selected for the collector Katherine S. Dreier in 1924 and which Ms. Dreier, in turn, had bequeathed to the Phillips at her death in 1952. The proceeds were to be added to the Phillips's general endowment. Once again, the AAMD, referring to its code of professional practices, pointed out that to use the proceeds in this manner would violate the standards it had promulgated for art museums.

While the Phillips ultimately did proceed with the sale—*Le Violon* was auctioned at Sotheby's in New York on 11 November 1987 for $3 million plus the 10-percent buyer's premium—it agreed to a compromise on the proposed use of the monies it received. These, it said, would be kept together as a fund for future acquisitions. Whatever income was generated pending such use would be applied exclusively to the care and maintenance of the permanent collection.

Another rule almost universally observed is that, notwithstanding that the approval of its board of trustees or other governing body will ultimately be required, the impetus for deaccessioning should initially come from those most immediately responsible for a museum's collection, i.e., from its curatorial staff and director. This is consistent with the rationale that deaccessioning should be employed solely to benefit the museum's collection, not in order to help it meet its operating budget. In the catalogue for a 1982 auction of some 700 works of art and other objects sold by the Los Angeles County Museum of Art "to benefit new acquisitions," its director gave the following description of that museum's deaccessioning process:

> So that it may . . . maintain the level of quality expected by a community which is expanding rapidly in knowledge and sophistication, the Museum unceasingly reviews and studies all works of art in its possession, periodically subjecting them to strict scrutiny to determine their condition, their art historical importance, their value to the permanent collection, and their utility to the community. . . . The criteria for deaccessioning are many: An artist or culture may be represented by more important examples; the Museum may have a large number of objects of one type or period and be entirely lacking in representation of other types or periods; or some works may no longer meet the standard of quality which rises as the collection grows.

A further self-imposed restriction in some museums—the Hirshhorn Museum is one—discourages the deaccessioning of work by a living artist without the artist's prior approval. At the Museum of Modern Art a similar policy extends to American artists only. Such policies are intended, out of common courtesy, to protect the artist's livelihood. Exceptions might be made—the Hirshhorn has made several: it did, for example, dispose at auction of a duplicate cast of Henry Moore's large *Seated Woman* in May 1986, several months before the sculptor's death— but only when the artist's reputation and market appear so secure that such a transaction should not cause these any damage.

The predominant practice among American museums is to channel the proceeds from deaccessioned works of art into their general acquisitions funds. In a few museums, however, such funds may be earmarked for an even more narrow purpose. At the Philadelphia Museum of Art, for example, curators are urged to replace a deaccessioned work of art with one of approximately equal value that might continue to carry the name as well as reflect the interests of the original donor.

In other museums, this procedure is reversed by having the acquisition decision *precede* the deaccessioning one. If the funds to acquire an important object are to be raised through deaccessioning, then this second approach often requires that the works chosen to be deaccessioned should be as close in period and medium as may be practical to the work to be acquired. Thus, in order to acquire two paintings from Claude Monet's haystack series, the Art Institute of Chicago sold two lesser works by Monet as well as several others by Pierre-Auguste Renoir. In a similar vein, when the Solomon R. Guggenheim Museum acquired its marble version of Constantin Brancusi's 1912 sculpture *The Muse* in 1985, the funds to cover its cost were raised in part by selling a plaster version of *The Muse* acquired some years earlier. Also sold were what the museum considered to be lesser works by several other important sculptors of the period including Raymond Duchamp-Villon and Jacques Lipchitz. Likewise, to help underwrite its 1987 purchase of *Seguidilla*, a key 1919 work in mixed media by Man Ray, the Hirshhorn Museum and Sculpture Garden deaccessioned a group of other works by the same artist that the director and curatorial staff had judged to be relatively less significant.

While auction sales have become the primary means through which most museums dispose of deaccessioned works of art, occasions may arise when a mutually beneficial exchange can be arranged. A dramatic instance of this occurred in 1982 when the Museum of Modern Art surrendered important paintings by Pablo Picasso and Henri Matisse to the Guggenheim in exchange for two paintings by Wassily Kandinsky. Through this exchange, the Modern was able to complete the ensemble of Kandinsky's four-painting suite, *Four Seasons*, while the Guggenheim was, at the same time, able to fill certain gaps in its collection. As the two museums noted in a joint press release: "The exchange importantly strengthens the collection of each of the institutions with works by artists particularly well represented in the other."

Notwithstanding that deaccessioning has been able to produce such salutary results in American art museums, it still continues to encounter resistance. On what is this based? The arguments that it might constitute a breach of faith with past donors or discourage present ones do not seem persuasive. Restrictions placed upon their gifts by donors have legal consequences that museums cannot ignore. The first step in any deaccessioning process must always be to determine whether the work in question may be disposed of in a legally acceptable manner. If not, the process ends right there. As for present donors, the anecdotal evidence to date would tend to indicate that a well-managed programme of deaccessioning, one that is clear, purposeful and conducted with integrity, is just as likely to make a museum attractive to donors as otherwise.

Of greater weight is the argument of "fallibility"—that those responsible for deaccessioning a work of art may ultimately prove to have been mistaken, either as to the facts of its authorship or, more likely, in their judgment as to its quality or importance. While the possibility of factual error is real enough for museums with collections of earlier art—the spectre most commonly raised is that of the carelessly discarded Renaissance painting which, to the deaccessioning museum's utter and everlasting humiliation, subsequently turns out to have been from the hand of Leonardo da Vinci—it has little pertinence to modern or contemporary collections where questions of authorship rarely arise. Not so, however, with errors of judgment. These are a real and haunting possibility for every museum that deaccessions. Although such errors can never be wholly avoided, much can be done to minimize them. A good starting-point is another of the standards promulgated by the AAMD—that the procedure for the deaccession of a work of art be "at least as rigorous" as that for the acquisition of one. In most American museums, it is even more so. Decisions to deaccession are, to the extent possible, made through a broad, deliberately paced and informed consensus, not hastily or by individual fiat. Moreover, if a deaccessioned work is to be disposed of by public sale, this fact is generally given broad advance publicity in order that dissenting views can come to the surface. Also widely observed is a principle that has long been enshrined in the Museum of Modern Art's formal deaccessioning policy: that a work of art must never be sold simply because the artist who created it is currently "out of fashion."

What must be understood in the end, however, is that it is exactly the same people that have been entrusted to build museum collections through selective acquisitions who are also responsible for the refining of those same collections through selective dispositions. If their judgment is considered trustworthy in the case of *accessioning*—if their perceptions of quality and importance are what a museum relies upon to commit its slender and very precious acquisitions funds—then why should there be such scepticism about their judgment in the case of *deaccessioning*?

During a lively debate over deaccessioning practices conducted at the 1987 meeting of The Council of Australian Museum Associations in Brisbane, it was forceful reiteration of exactly this question by Patrick McCaughey—then director of the National Gallery of Victoria—that carried the day against the "fallibility" argument advanced by the opposing side. In a similar vein, one veteran American museum official recently noted: ". . . it is the same eyes that sell well or poorly as those that buy well or poorly. The director or curator who does not know how to sell probably does not know how to buy."

Errors of commission are potentially inherent in any programme of deaccessioning. Those who focus on that possibility rarely discuss, however, the equal potential for errors of omission that is inherent in the process of acquiring. In theory, it should make no difference to the ultimate shape of a museum's collection if an important work of art was never purchased at all or if, having once been purchased, it was thereafter sold through poor judgment. Either way, the museum is without it.

In actual fact, however, the number of important artworks that have failed ever to enter a museum's collection because somebody, whether for lack of judgment, opportunity, courage or the necessary funds, failed to buy them in the first place must exceed by many a dozen the number of important artworks that have been removed from such collections because somebody disposed of them in error. While deaccessioning is not without its dangers, we have found—in America, at least, and at least for museums of modern and contemporary art—that the risks it poses are not unmanageable and that the rewards it offers can be very great.

Deaccessioning in American Museums: II — Some Thoughts for England

By Michael Conforti

At a recent American art historical conference Joseph Rykwert upheld his reputation for non-conformist views by suggesting that there is a revisionism at play in contemporary society that will eventually alter the cult-like status which art museums have attained in Western culture. The former Cambridge professor, now professor of architecture at the University of Pennsylvania, sees evidence that our society is "taking the work of art out of the museum and returning it to its proper usage in the marketplace." For Rykwert, "It is, in a sentence, a program for a century."[1]

Professor Rykwert's perspective regarding the slow dismantling of museums' collections would send shudders through the English and American art community if they felt his vision had any possibility of being realized. In fact, recently, his perspectives regarding art's rightful place in commerce have been supported by certain museum practices, spurred on by a buoyant international art market and the conservative fiscal policies of the world's two principal Anglo states. Rumblings in the British Parliament regarding the sale of museum collections to fund ever more expensive operating costs have only gone into abeyance, not disappeared,[2] while American institutions seem to be in a frenzy to sell all works of questionable collection status, but definite market value. Each museum consignment to auction

Michael Conforti is director of the Sterling and Francine Clark Art Institute, Williamstown, Mass. An expert on sculpture and decorative arts, he frequently writes on 19th- and 20th-century private and institutional collecting. "Deaccessioning in American Museums: II—Some Thoughts for England" first appeared in the August 1989 issue of APOLLO *magazine. Reproduced courtesy of* APOLLO *magazine.*

is catalyzed by unprecedented recent auction prices, and the psychological and real effect of the U.S. government's abolition of significant tax benefits to donors of works of art.[3] The four weeks from the first of May to early June 1989, were a bonanza for the New York auction rooms. In no similar period in America's history have so many museums sold so many paintings so openly—and with so little accompanying controversy.[4]

This current wave of deaccessioning is hardly the first in museum history. The paintings which left the Hermitage in the 1930s, when Andrew Mellon bought 33 works for a reported $19 million, eased the Russian balance of payments and helped establish the National Gallery of Art in Washington. Germany was also caught in a financial bind after World War I and sent a number of works from various museums to market. More paintings left when Hitler's aesthetic ideology removed modernist art from public collections. In England, too, Dulwich, the British Museum, the National Gallery and the Victoria and Albert Museum have all sold works in the past, but England has never sold in quantity. Professional dissatisfaction with the effects of past sales discredited deaccessioning in England by the early 1970s.[5]

Of all Western countries America is the most experienced in the practice of deaccessioning publicly entrusted works of art. In the years following World War II, American institutions stepped up their earlier practice of refinement and modernization in a series of aggressive sales. In New York, Philadelphia, Minneapolis and many other cities, collections left institutions *en bloc* as unfashionable objects were cashed in to improve permanent collections. Minneapolis's sales were among the most infamous of the 1950s. Four thousand five hundred items of decorative and oriental art; American paintings; and Egyptian, Greek and Roman works of art were sold in the hope of achieving a collection of masterpieces with an emphasis on late 19th- and 20th-century European modernism.[6]

After a lull in deaccessioning activity caused by the negative publicity over the 1950s sales, another wave of selling followed in the early 1970s, led by the Metropolitan Museum of Art. Again, however, the public and media reacted. The sale of a Rousseau and a van Gogh from the collection of Adelaide de Groot and the exchange of six of her modern masters (one Modigliani, two Juan Gris, a Bonnard, a Picasso and a Renoir) for a David Smith and a Richard Diebenkorn became nothing less than an international scandal. Articles and books were written chastising Thomas Hoving for his deaccessioning practices and the attorney general of New York reprimanded the museum publicly.[7]

In the mid-1970s, museums throughout the country curtailed their selling activities as each drafted deaccessioning policies with a new consciousness of their legal responsibilities and of the charges of unprofessional behaviour that might be levelled against them. While the law did not require it, many new policies stated that donors or heirs of donors were to be notified of sales if possible. Their names would also be transferred to a newly acquired work, followed with the words "by exchange." In 1981, the Association of Art Museum Directors (AAMD) published a statement against the sale of works of art to fund operating costs.[8] In the last 15 years legal seminars and articles have articulated accepted deaccessioning practices for all American public institutions, while at the same time stressing an administrator's responsibility for "collections management," often citing the cost of maintaining any object in a museum storeroom.[9]

While curatorial professionals in any American museum are quick to point out the mistakes inherent in previous institutional sales, the heavy silence over current deaccessioning activity suggests that many believe this generation to be fully educated as to the pitfalls of the practice, and that it is coping intelligently and pragmatically with the demands of a new administrative and fiscal climate. Certainly, with institutional policies now in place and "collections management" considered an intelligent goal of every museum administration, the legal foundation and professional justifications for deaccessioning activities are stronger than at any time in the past.[10] In this environment objects must now be accountable to a system in which collections not on view are considered of questionable institutional value. The new breed of entrepreneurial trustee guiding many American museums is quick to make operational comparisons with his own market-driven, profit-making organization: Storage is often considered "dead inventory," visible to few, an institutional asset waiting to be struck from the debit side of the ledger and turned into cash.

This view is reinforced by changes in the art market, combined with new American tax laws, which have altered the museums' confidence in their collecting and operating future. Trustees and professionals watch helplessly as wills are rewritten and long-expected collections march to auction.[11] They are aware that even a return of the appreciated gift deduction will not counter the effect of the prices attained for certain Old Master, Impressionist and modern works. News of auction activity has become of national interest, and the media keep every trustee, professional and member of the public fully informed of record prices. It is now widely believed that if long-desired works are ever to be acquired, they must be found and purchased quickly—and works of art may have to be sold to pay for them. In contrast with past practice, an institution's name is now consistently used to help promote the sale. A backlash from future donors seems no longer a concern, for they, too, it would seem, understand the necessity of the current frenzy.

In addition to deaccessioning with the ultimate goal of either cleaning out storage or producing cash, there are other justifications:[12] Most institutions accept the wisdom of selling severely damaged objects. Duplicates, too, are considered saleable by even the most conservative organizations, although the definition of a duplicate varies from one museum to another.[13]

When a museum changes its collection mission, enormously valuable objects can be made available for sale. In the recent past the Kimbell Art Museum has chosen not to include Old Master drawings within the scope of its collection.[14] Minnesota's Walker Art Center changed its focus to contemporary art many years ago and recently decided to continue deaccessioning the original T. B. Walker Collection to enhance its endowment for 20th-century purchases.[15] The Pennsylvania Academy of Fine Arts and the Corcoran Gallery in Washington, both formerly rich in European and American 19th-century paintings, chose to sell their European pictures recently and concentrate exclusively on American works.[16] The Corcoran's Frederich Kaemmerer, acquired by the museum's founder from the artist the year after it was exhibited at the Paris Salon of 1874, set a record for the artist at auction.[17] Realizing that a group of works by Georgia O'Keeffe were regularly on view at the nearby Amon Carter Museum, O'Keeffe's *Yellow Cactus Flowers* of 1929 was recently consigned to auction by the Modern Art Museum of Fort Worth.[18] Many considered this move an intelligent decision in asset management as the market in Georgia O'Keeffe's works is currently being fuelled by a popular monograph exhibition travelling across the country.

As the AAMD has frowned on sales to support operating costs, art museums, for the most part, have followed their recommendation. When institutions consider this avenue, as the New-York Historical Society did recently, they are often subject to active criticism by the American press.[19] The conservation of collections is now however, interpreted as being non-operational, a point of view which supported recent sales from the Henry Ford Museum and the Phillips Collection in Washington.[20] Smaller, badly funded museums and historic houses seem to feel more justified in selling works to enhance operations endowments.[21] Indeed, the most spectacular sale ever of a piece of American furniture was in order to establish such an endowment. The Nicholas Brown desk and bookcase was sold for the benefit of the John Nicholas Brown Center for the Study of American Civilization sited in the Brown family house, Providence, R.I.[22] The highboy had stood in this late 18th-century house since 1814, but the institution decided that a substantial operations endowment represented a better way of serving the center than maintaining the object in its original family environment.

But by far the strongest motive for selling by American museums is to refine or upgrade collections. American collections are by and large representative in nature and a quest for "masterpiece" works to represent an artist or an artistic movement often underlies the collecting mission of most institutions.[23] Generally, when an American museum refines its collection, one or more works are recommended for sale with proceeds held for later translation into a single "better" work for exhibition, sometimes in the same field, sometimes not. The money yielded from the pictures recently sold by the Kimbell Art Museum, for example, will presumably pay for objects more consistent with the "masterpiece" aspirations of its collection.[24] In large museums, sale income is often earmarked for acquisitions by the curatorial department from which objects were sold. Occasionally, institutional restrictions try to maintain the character of the original collection; at the Wadsworth Atheneum in Hartford, Conn., there has to be a similarity in medium, period and style between any object sold and any object acquired. Restrictions preserving the historical character of a collection are rare, however.

Considerable income can result from a museum changing its collecting policy, as generally acknowledged masterpieces can be eliminated from the newly adopted scope of the collection. Few members of the public are capable of arguing against a change in collecting mission for the potential pitfalls are hard to measure at the time of sale: Is the institution sacrificing its future collection or its cultural responsibility through over-confidence in present day taste or current institutional perspectives; will the exchange made with the deaccessioning funds continue to be considered aesthetically or monetarily equal over time? At some point in the future, Texas might want to have a collection of drawings to complement the Kimbell's paintings. The next generation may wish to examine European works known to Philadelphia's artists in the context of the Pennsylvania Academy's collection, or relate William Corcoran's European paintings to the American works he bought at the same time. The public museums in Minneapolis-St. Paul maintain the most insignificant collection of American 19th-century paintings of virtually any metropolitan centre in the country; the sale of the Walker Art Center's pictures will help to insure this position forever.

The only immediately obvious mistake any institution has to fear is where a curator's recommendation conflicts with the market's valuation of a deaccessioned work. This can lose the institution money, undermine public confidence, and even lead to legal action. The recent sales of American furniture by the Henry Ford Museum were the most publicized example of such a misjudgment. An American sofa that was sold for $16,500 at an auction house in Chicago (an unlikely marketplace for American furniture) was placed in a well-known New York gallery for $1 million.[25] When any former museum painting is offered for sale in a Bond Street gallery, the museum has to defend the fact of having sold it against the learned rhetoric of the dealer who must present it as a masterpiece, and also against the huge mark-up in price that is now claimed to be its value.

As mentioned earlier, the current situation in museum deaccessioning is driven by an inflationary art market and pressures to manage collections more efficiently, but it is supported by new attitudes towards education in the museum environment as well. It was a belief in the educational, as well as moral and aesthetic values associated with works of art that spawned many European museums in the 19th century. That belief catalyzed American civic leaders into the establishment of art museums in the United States. At first the museums' educational mission encouraged broadly based collections which put the works into a visual context (this was particularly true in applied arts museums like the South Kensington Museum (now the Victoria and Albert), the paradigm for many early American museum initiatives). By a context, early educational theorists meant the exhibition of works next to those of corresponding nature. Today, however, it tends to mean a didactic explanation within a framework of social and economic history, and the need for associating objects with other objects is perceived to be less vital. Furthermore, the vision of a museum collection as an aesthetic library, an encyclopaedia of style, form and decoration, is not thought worth expressing today. Instead, it is assumed by the general public, as well as many museum professionals and trustees, that any objects not actually on exhibition, are merely "rotting away," being selfishly kept from public consumption by narrow-minded, hoarding curators.

It is a paradox that the deaccessioning fever comes at a time when many art historians are expanding the canon of works of art, allowing objects little considered in the past to share cultural and aesthetic reinterpretation with long accepted masterworks. Collections as a whole are also considered objects of study today,[26] and more than one paper at recent art historical conventions has focused on the museum itself as a cultural artefact.[27] These expansionist views, however, have had little effect on the actions of art museums, whose collecting mission is currently interpreted as to improve and refine what is already in the collections while creating a more efficient operation in the process—the aesthetic imperative in a pragmatic world.

In the current climate every object must be accountable, but collections in store are not a useless institutional appendage. Many storage areas contain collections of quality awaiting future gallery space, and even fakes or reproductions have educational value in institutions. Storage can also be made more "accountable" to its audience when a museum is willing to invest in "open storage," accessible to the public. The most successful recently completed study/storage is the Henry Luce Center of American Art at the Metropolitan Museum where American paintings and decorative arts are attractively, but efficiently, crowded behind glass enclosures. Labels are simple, but computer terminals are placed nearby for public access to further information.

But the drive to deaccession will continue in America until another obvious mistake is detected by the media, resulting perhaps in some state attorney general raising the issue with the museum's board of trustees. American museums will then curtail the sale of works of art for a period of years, until memories have faded and the practice resumes.

The see-saw will continue for practical and cultural reasons. America's public art collections have been treated pragmatically throughout their history.[28] America's museums, like most of its cultural organizations, are privately sponsored and endowed, civically supported entities whose mission can be adapted to many organizational or civic needs. Except, maybe, for the National Gallery of Art (where deaccessioning is not allowed), no art museum is thought to represent a national cultural patrimony and there is little legislation forming a federal cultural policy. While standard practices are widely communicated through the country's professional associations, deaccessioning is rarely presented, as it should be, in the context of deeply considered thought regarding the place of a permanent collection of art in American culture—the professional guidelines are legal and procedural, rather than philosophical in tone.[29] This is in keeping with the character of the country. America may be the centre of ideological pragmatism; it is certainly a place where change is an assumption and "modern" a permanent value. It is a country which has achieved its position in the world through a lack of historical consciousness and a readiness to deal creatively with the traditions it has inherited. One could argue that it is appropriate that America's public art collections reflect this cultural reality as works flow in and out of its museums from generation to generation.

In the meantime one sees England looking to America for guidance on how to reshape its museums. In the area of deaccessioning it should be careful not to take an inappropriate American model and misapply it as has been done regularly in the recent past.[30]

The foundation and public expectation of the American museum differs sharply from its English counterpart. While the American museum grew out of a 19th-century English museological model, its evolution has been different in its funding, its legal relationship to government and its collection mission. The English national museums not only reflect the country's educational, moral and aesthetic values of the last 150 or more years, but their collections have become national cultural patrimony. This status is assumed in their funding by government, in their organizational structure and in the attitude of the English people towards the objects in their care. The deaccessioning of works of art which are generally perceived as representing the national heritage has many more pitfalls to it than it would have in America, especially when loans to provincial museums can be presented as an alternative. "Collecting accountability" does not justify sales as there is little money to be raised from most of what is in store. If England wants to raise money for museum operations, it must consider seriously what one prominent English museum director once jokingly suggested—the sale of a Leonardo or a Michelangelo from a national collection, which could support an institution for decades. If it is in this direction that the Thatcherites in Parliament want to turn to raise money for operations, they should be willing to stand and defend such an act.

Rather than causing the controversy which would result from the misapplication of American deaccessioning practices, Britain should consider the example of its Common Market partners, France or Germany, when remodelling its museums. At a time when, as Joseph Rykwert so rightly tells us, museums are the quasi-religious cult centres of our society, France is currently capitalizing on the long-standing relationship between its national pride and national collections. The Louvre renovation is only the latest expression of a cultural policy formed to enhance the image of the state, a policy which has served the French well since the age of Louis XIV. With the completion of the Beaubourg, the Orsay, and now the new Louvre, tourism is thriving as crowds line up to pay hefty admission prices and buy the trinkets everyone must have to remember their visit to the shrine. The respect derived from these self-confident museum enterprises has made France more of a driving force in international culture than at any other time in recent memory.

Since the 17th century, England's cultural life has been bound up in a tradition of collecting and connoisseurship, a tradition second to none in the Western world. From the eclectic Grand Tour assemblages kept in its most famous country houses to the teapot and treen collections in country cottages, art collecting has been an integral part of England's history, its national heritage and its sense of itself as a people. This remarkable tradition cannot be overlooked as the country reforms its cultural policy to meet the fiscal problems of the coming decades. One fears, however, the shopkeeping mentality of the current parliamentary majority may not be up to the task. Instead they seem to be moving towards support of Professor Rykwert's conservative dream—the banishing of public art to the marketplace. If parliamentary rhetoric were put into action, it may not take a century to get the job done.

Notes

1. Rykwert's perspectives were presented at a symposium, "Reading Art Museums," organized by John Walsh at the College Art Association annual meeting, San Francisco, February 1989. See also, Joseph Rykwert, "The Cult of the Museum," *The Architect and Design Review of Houston*, fall 1988, pp. 16-18. For assistance with this reference and other research for this article, I want to thank Scott Amacker of the Minneapolis Institute of Arts.

2. For example, "Art Gallery Move Opposed by Peers," London *Times*, 4 March 1988. Simon Jenkins, "A Treasure Trove, Rotting in the Attic," London *Times.* 1 May 1988; Patricia Morison, "Bargains in the Basement?," *The Daily Telegraph*, 6 June 1988.

3. See Michael Kimmelman, "The Case of the Vanishing Art," *The New York Times*, 14 May 1989, Section 2, p. 1; also Lee Rosenbaum, "The Anxious Acquisitors," *ARTnews*, March 1989, pp. 144-51.

4. The following list (and total dollars realized) represents paintings sold by American museums at Christie's and Sotheby's, New York, from 1 May to 3 June 1989: Walker Art Center, Minneapolis, 17 ($12,597,200); Metropolitan Museum of Art, New York, 13 ($12,055,450); Chrysler Museum of Art, Norfolk, Va., 7 ($2,755,300); Philadelphia Museum of Art, 6 ($2,965,000); Kimbell Art Museum, Fort Worth, Tex., 4 ($2,237,400); Art Institute of Chicago, 3 ($4,620,000); Brooklyn Museum of Art, N.Y., 3 ($1,980,000); The Wadsworth Atheneum, Hartford, Conn., 3 ($203,500); Cincinnati Art Museum, Ohio, 2 ($880,000);

Modern Art Museum of Fort Worth, Tex., 1 ($1,320,000); The Sheldon Museum, Middlebury, Vt., 1 ($242,000); Newport Harbor Art Museum, Newport Beach, Calif., 1 ($82,500); New Museum of Contemporary Art, New York, 1 ($41,250); North Carolina Museum of Art, Raleigh, and the Ackland Art Museum, Chapel Hill, N.C., 1 ($9,900).

5. See John Jacob and A. Kenneth Snowman, "The Sale or Disposal of Museum Objects," *Museums Journal*, XI , no. 3, 3 December 1971, pp. 112-16.

6. See Jeffrey Hess, *Their Splendid Legacy: The First 100 Years of the Minneapolis Society of Fine Arts*, 1985, pp. 62-64.

7. John Rewald, "Should Hoving be De-accessioned?," *Art in America*, LXI, no. 1, January 1973, pp. 24-30; John Hess, *The Grand Acquisitors*, 1974. For the attorney general's statement, see J. Merryman and A. Elsen, *Law, Ethics and the Visual Arts: Cases and Materials*, 1979, II, pp. 7, 144-47, 158.

8. Their statement reads: "The deaccession and disposal of a work of art from a museum's collection requires particularly rigorous examination. Deaccessioning should be related to policy rather than to the exigencies of the moment, and funds obtained through disposal must be used to replenish the collection." *Professional Practices in Art Museums: Report of the Ethics and Standards Committee*, American Association of Art Museum Directors, 1981, pp. 11-12.

9. F. Feldman & S. Weil, *Art Works: Law, Policy, Practice, Practising Law Institute*, 1974, pp. 1113-1134; American Association of Museums, "Museum Ethics," *Museum News*, LVI, no. 4, March/April 1978, pp. 21-30; M. Malaro, "Collections Management Policies," *Museum News*, LVIII, no. 2, Nov./Dec. 1979, pp. 57-61; M. Phelan, *Museums and the Law*, Nashville, Tenn: The American Association for State and Local History, 1982, pp. 240-42; M. Malaro, "Deaccessioning: The Importance of Procedure," *Museum News*, LVIII, no. 2, March/April 1988, pp. 74-75; ALI/ABA (American Law Institute-American Bar Association) Course of Study Materials, "Legal Problems in Museums Administration," 1989, pp. 396-98.

10. The current trend of considering deaccessioning solely in legal and procedural terms contrasts sharply with the ethical and historical perspectives expressed in the mid-1970s in the wake of the Metropolitan sales. See, for example, Egbert H. Begemann, "The Price is Never Right," *Museum News*, LI, no. 9, May 1973, pp. 32-35; Michael O'Hare and Alan L. Feld, "Is Museum Speculation in Art Immoral, Illegal and Insufficiently Fattening?," *Museum News*, LIII, no. 8, May 1975, pp. 24ff.

11. Collections associated with museums which were sold in May in New York include Chicago's Searle Collection (Christie's, 10 May 1989) and Los Angeles's Wallis Collection (Christie's, 10 May 1989). The Jacopo Pontormo, long on view at the Frick, was auctioned to endow a nonprofit foundation (Sotheby's, 31 May 1989). Also, the change in the will of long-time Philadelphia trustee John Dorrance in the wake of new tax laws had disastrous financial consequences for the Philadelphia Museum of Art. See Grace Glueck, "Donations of Art Fall Sharply After Changes in the Tax Code," *The New York Times*, 1 May 1989.

12. Deaccessioning motives rarely have been discussed as openly as in the panel discussion by four American decorative arts curators transcribed in Myrna Kaye, "Deaccessioning: The Curator's Problems," *Maine Antique Digest*, XV, no. 9, September 1987, pp. 10ff. and XV, no. 10, October 1987, pp. 10ff.

13. The strictest view would allow only coins from the same die and prints of the same state to be considered a duplication. This view, for example, is incorporated into the British Museum's policy of deaccessioning.

14. Sotheby's, London, 6 July 1987.

15. Sotheby's, New York, 24 May 1989.

16. European paintings belonging to the Pennsylvania Academy recently appeared in the following Christie's New York sales: 28 May 1988; 20 October 1988; 11 January 1989; 23 February 1989. For the most recent Corcoran sales, see Sotheby's, New York, 27 October 1988; 7 April 1989.

17. Sotheby's, 27 October 1988, lot 88.

18. Sotheby's, New York, 24 May 1989, lot 217.

19. Douglas McGill, "Criticism Moves the Historial Society, a Little," *The New York Times*, 25 July 1988, C13, C15 (L).

20. For the recent Ford sales see Sandra Rubin Tessler, "Harold Skramstad and the Strife at Henry Ford Museum," *Michigan*, 26 July 1987, pp. 8-17. The sale of the Philips Collection's George Braque (Sotheby's, New York, 11 November 1987, lot 46) to support "curatorial expenses—conservation, research and installation" was defended by its director in Lee Rosenbaum, op. cit., p. 150.

21. The Sheldon Museum in Middlebury, Vt., recently sold its Frederic Church *On Otter Creek* to benefit the museum's endowment fund (Sotheby's, 24 May 1989, lot 52).

22. Sotheby's, New York, 3 June 1989, lot 100.

23. This goal is frequently discredited by European museum curators for whom the contexts provided by complimentary works are seen as an equal, if not over-rriding, collecting objective. In a rare instance of an American museum selling works to concentrate on a contextual display, judicious sales of certain Impressionist paintings from the Art Institute of Chicago in the mid-1980s recreated a series of Monet's *Haystacks* for the permanent collection.

24. Sotheby's, New York, 2 June 1989, lots 93-100.

25. Leslie Hindman, Chicago, 7 December 1986, lot 86.

26. *The Journal of the History of Collections* was begun this year, published by Oxford University Press.

27. For example, a session "The Art Museum as Artifact" was organized for the College Art Association's 1987 annual meeting in Boston.

28. Collections in America have even been bequeathed to museums with the assumption of future refinements. The Winterbotham Collection at the Art Institute of Chicago was designated as a "rotating" collection by the donor in the 1930s. Proceeds from works sold go towards subsequent additions. Two paintings from this collection, a Kokoschka and a Soutine, were sold in New York in May for a total of $3,850,000 (Sotheby's, 9 May 1989, lot 34; Christie's, 10 May 1989, lot 67).

29. The mood in the United States may be changing in light of recent deaccessioning activity, however. In discussing the Pontormo sale, journalist Michael Kimmelman recently raised the question "How are we to define what is culturally

valuable to us as a nation and what are we willing to do to protect it?" *The New York Times*, 3 June 1989, p. 12 (R).

30. The trend began with expensive "blockbuster" shows before corporate funding of exhibitions in England reached its current level of success. It was followed soon by inappropriately placed retail initiatives, shop barricades in the centre of museum entrances (only some later moved to side galleries). The misunderstood American model is particularly apparent in the initiatives recently taken to revitalize the V & A (Victoria and Albert Museum of Art). American trustees are not political appointments, as they appear to be in the new V & A system (and U.S. counterparts are expected to give substantially to support operating costs). American art museums are not guided by people without a background in art history. The American museums' well-known commitment to retailing would still fall short of the loan of museum objects to department stores. And no American art museum would consider promoting the auction of a pop singer's memorabilia as an exhibition in its galleries, a misguided attempt to attract crowds that undermines public confidence in the museum's ability to carry out its mission.

The Deaccession Cookie Jar

By Stephen E. Weil

Should a museum be able to apply the proceeds from deaccessioning to meet some part of its operating expenses, or must its use of such funds be restricted—as many museum codes now require—to the replenishment of its collection?

Recent discussions concerning these alternatives have focused primarily on issues of legality, ethics, and professional standards. Boards of trustees and other governing authorities that find themselves confronting this question should understand, however, that how they respond may have important strategic implications as well. These implications extend well beyond the most immediate effect of such a decision, i.e., that observance of the replenishment rule will leave a museum's "capital" intact, whereas the use of deaccessioning proceeds to meet some part of its operating expenses will diminish the museum's underlying resources.

In brief, the museum that evidences its willingness to apply deaccessioning proceeds to meet operating expenses may ultimately be perceived, both by its community and its staff, to have made available to itself the functional equivalent of a cash reserve, a reserve equal in amount to the total market value of its collection. The consequences of such a perception may, in turn, have a significant impact on many of the most important aspects of its operations.

Before examining these consequences in greater detail, two background observations may be in order. First, museums—like most nonprofit organizations, governments included—are under continuous

"The Deaccession Cookie Jar" originally appeared in the November/December 1992 issue of Museum News, *published by AAM.*

pressure to expend to the very fullest whatever resources they may currently have available. A nonprofit organization that accumulates or maintains unrestricted reserves may be viewed (and not merely by the public, but by the Internal Revenue Service as well) as not doing all that it possibly can do to carry out its charitable purpose. In consequence, most such organizations sooner or later tend to operate near (and sometimes even beyond) the edge of their available resources. To be hard-pressed for operating funds is the chronic and natural condition of most nonprofit organizations. Second, in the particular case of museums, there is a grotesque disproportion between the estimated market values of their collections and the funds which they generally have available to meet their operating needs.

According to the American Association of Museums' data report from the *1989 National Museum Survey*, the total fiscal year 1988 operating expenses of museums in the United States (after excluding such related but non-object-collecting organizations as aquariums, arboreta, planetariums, and zoos) was approximately $3.3 billion. These museums held just over 700 million objects in their collections. Assuming—after averaging ploughshares and paintings, bedsteads and bugs—that these 700 million collection objects had an average market value of just $100 each, then their total value would have been upward of $70 billion. To take the art museums alone, if the average market value of the 13 million objects which they owned as of 1988 was as little as $5,000 each, then the total value of their holdings would still be at least $65 billion. Such collection values not only dwarf the funds which these museums have available for operations, but also are considerably greater than their combined endowment funds, calculated in the data report to be just under $14 billion.

Against such a background, what attitudinal and behavioral consequences might museums expect—both externally and internally—if and when their publics and staff once began to perceive that this enormous value was not permanently set aside in the form of their collections but was potentially available to be used to meet their current operating expenses?

The external consequences seem plain enough. Virtually every museum is engaged in a constant competition with other charitable organizations of every kind for the scarce resources of public funding, foundation grants, corporate sponsorship, and private contributions. While the degree of an organization's need may only be one factor in determining how successfully it can compete, the public's perception that a museum is able to help itself through sales from its collection must inevitably make it a less appealing candidate for outside support than an equally worthwhile organization that has no such capacity for self-help. How long, for example, might the taxpayers of a community tolerate the use of their money to help support the operation of a local museum that was perceived as readily able to provide its own support by simply making a few additional sales from its collection? In these circumstances, might not many other community needs appear to be more compelling?

Not only do museums compete for support, they are also themselves at the center of a second kind of competition, a competition among those who look to them for the delivery of program services. The demands for such services can take many forms. A nearby retirement home would like an outreach program. The local school system is requesting more teacher training. A distant neighborhood would like a satellite facility. Under normal circumstances, a museum's ability to respond positively to all of these competing demands will be constrained by the limited resources it has available. Program proposals must compete with one another, and only a handful can eventually be funded.

The perception that a museum's collection constituted the equivalent of a significant cash reserve could transform that situation entirely. So long as the museum was perceived as a "deep pocket," there would be little to constrain the demand for new programs. Such demands might even be expected to grow. More ominously, such proposed new programs would not merely compete (as they do now) with one another, but also would compete with the objects that still remained in the museum's collection. The argument to be expected—and it would most certainly be an argument conducted in the media—would be one that involved the relative value of people and things. Is the retention of the museum's fourth-best Rembrandt etching really more important that a proposed new program for preschoolers? Might not the disposal of one old fire engine be a truly modest price to pay in order to keep the museum open to the public three evenings a week? More often that not, when a public argument is framed in terms of living people against dead things, the living people can be expected to win.

Internally, the consequences of the use of deaccessioning proceeds to meet operating expenses might in some ways be parallel. Staff members also compete with one another in putting forward program proposals. Economic constraints dictate that only a few such proposals can be adopted at any time. Except for an iron self-discipline, what would stand in the way of the museum that had seemingly unlimited resources from putting into place virtually every worthy program its staff could generate? More to the point, absent such an iron self-discipline, for how long would those resources remain unlimited?

A second internal consequence might involve staff compensation. To the extent that museum workers generally consider themselves (and frequently with ample reason) to be underpaid compared to their peers in the for-profit sector, on what grounds could their requests for more equitable compensation be resisted when the entire value of the museum's collection was available to support such compensation? Once again, the issue might be framed as people against things, and once again the more likely loser would be the things.

Regardless, however, of whether deaccessioning proceeds were used to increase staff salaries or merely to continue them at current levels, their use for this purpose—almost invariably the case in museums when "operating expenses" are at issue, since salaries and benefits generally make up anywhere from one-half to two-thirds of such expenses—may raise a second ethical question. In terms of conflict of interest, what is the situation of a museum staff member who participates in a deaccessioning process that, as one of its end results, enables that staff member to continue to receive a salary that he or she might have otherwise lost? For that matter, might not a similar conflict of interest question be raised with respect to the member of a museum board or other governing body that initiated a deaccessioning process which, as one of its end results, discharged the board's duty to secure the resources necessary to maintain the institution?

Without preaching the virtues of poverty, it might still be argued that the austerity with which most museums in the United States have been forced to operate in recent years has imposed its own kind of managerial discipline. That museums have been successful in learning to do as much as they do with constantly diminished resources has been a strong argument for continued public confidence. Could such discipline be maintained if museums were understood by their boards and staff alike to be in possession of a vast cash reserve that could always be used to the extent necessary to offset any extravagance, waste, or error? That collections can be used in such a way is not farfetched. When Edinburgh University auctioned off its complete edition of Audubon's *Birds of America* in the spring of 1992, the proceeds were intended to cover a multimillion-dollar shortfall resulting from the university's immediately prior miscalculation of its anticipated revenues.

If this analysis has merit, then it may be an illusion to think that a museum faced with a shortage of operating funds can rectify that situation through the use of deaccessioning proceeds. Whatever relief such proceeds may provide is likely to be short-term at best. Once the barrier of a strictly observed replenishment rule has been breached, there may be compelling pressures—from both outside and inside the museum—to breach it repeatedly. Considered as a cookie jar, a museum collection has the peculiarity that, once the lid is removed, it may prove impossible ever to get it permanently back in place.

The museum that finds itself short of operating funds but still with its collection intact, and still with at least a modicum of hope that the support it needs may be available tomorrow if not today, may find that in the end—by recurring raids on that collection—it will still be short of operating funds, but with its collection long gone and with no plausible reason remaining as to why the public ought to support it further. Legality, ethics, and professional standards aside, the use of deaccessioning proceeds to meet a museum's operating expenses would appear to be an inherently self-defeating strategy. Worse, to the extent that such a use may affect the public's perception of not just one museum but all museums, it may also constitute a distinct threat to the entire community of museums.

"Guilt-Free" Deaccessioning

By Steven H. Miller

Museums exist to preserve objects of cultural and scientific importance. This function makes them unique. It permeates virtually every aspect of their operations, from collecting to conservation to scholarship and exhibition.

Acquiring collections is the first preservation action museums take. Following this critical step, other related tasks commence. The preservation imperative is a ceaseless one. As public trust stewards, museums strive to retain collections in perpetuity. Yet, occasionally museums need to remove collections. First in use in the early 1970s, the word describing such activity is "deaccessioning." It has become one of the most, if not *the* most, controversial museum practices.

Deaccessioning takes place for many reasons ranging from the obvious and logical to the weak and bizarre. Museums deaccession because items don't fit into a museum's collecting scope; proper care cannot be provided; items are in poor condition or pose a danger to people or other collections; objects are deemed of "lesser quality," are redundant, or exist in duplicate; collecting missions are altered; items can provide income; there is no interest in a collection; storage space is at a premium; curatorial tastes change; administrative priorities have altered.

The reasons museums give for removing collections can be discussed at length, and indeed they should be. But of equal importance is how deaccessioning occurs. Traditionally, collections are either giv-

Steven H. Miller is executive director of The Bennington Museum, Bennington, Vt. "'Guilt-Free' Deaccessioning" originally appeared in the September/October 1996 issue of Museum News, *published by AAM.*

en away, traded, destroyed, or sold. The first and second choices happen on occasion. The third is a fairly rare event. The fourth is by far the most familiar option. Yet, it is sale of museum artifacts on the open market that often results in tremendous and vitriolic controversy, probably because commercial sale seems to contradict basic museum preservation duties and to contravene public trust agreements implicit in donation or purchase transactions.

From a preservation perspective, sale on the open market can put objects in danger of physical and intellectual depredation. Items are separated from their histories, altered, and sometimes lost forever. This is hardly how museums are supposed to care for their collections. The public, and the press in particular, sees commercial sale as an abrogation of an almost sacred duty.

It is difficult to quantify perceptions of public trust violations that result when a museum sells something. The bonds of faith museums enjoy are often intangible. The damage that results from commercial deaccessioning is best explained in public relations terms. What potential donor will trust a museum that sells collections? How can museums garner sustained public support if they appear to inexplicably wander off course? Can the public believe that what they see in our museums is truly being cared for, for them and future generations? These are critical considerations if we understand that the vast majority of museum collections have been donated and that most museums survive on public good will.

On the other hand, museums need the collection management option that deaccessioning offers. There are legitimate reasons for removing collections, and viable avenues must be available to legally and practicably accomplish this task. The question is, can deaccessioning be done in a manner that upholds the preservation role that museums, by definition, assume? Is there a way to avoid the perils and pitfalls of commercial deaccessioning?

Inter-museum deaccessioning offers a positive answer to these questions. This option is achieved by transferring collections from one museum to another. The process can be carried out by gift, sale, exchange, or other equitable arrangement and can meet several extremely important goals. Collections are preserved and stay in the public sector. They remain accessible to scholars and general audiences. Museums sustain their reputation as keepers of shared material culture and scientific evidence. And institutions are freed of inappropriate collections that drain resources, allowing staff, space, and budget allocations to be assigned to higher priorities.

If inter-museum transfer is done responsibly, receiving institutions can greatly benefit from new acquisitions. These museums can better appreciate the collections, provide appropriate care, and offer improved intellectual custody. The collections that are transferred would also benefit. Properly cared for in museum custody, they would enjoy a much better chance of survival than if they were subjected to the vicissitudes of private ownership and the commercial market.

Inter-museum deaccessioning can be achieved in a number of ways. Museums may individually seek institutions to receive collections being removed. They can make contacts, hold discussions, and determine an appropriate arrangement. Museums may also approach the matter collaboratively. The National Park Service, for instance, has a central office that lists collections no longer needed along with those being sought. Sites within the park service are eligible to participate; museums outside the service may utilize the office on a case-by-case basis and as scheduling permits.

Within the past decade, there has been exciting precedent for inter-museum deaccessioning. In every case deaccessioned collections have remained in museums and thus are preserved and kept in the public sector. In 1984, for example, the Philadelphia Museum of Art and the Pennsylvania Academy of Fine Arts entered into a collection transfer agreement. First, the museum gave the academy a painting by American artist Charles Demuth and a certain sum of money in exchange for 2,400 European drawings. A year later, the academy gave the museum 43,000 Old Master and 19th-century European prints in exchange for six works of American art and an undisclosed financial contribution.

In the course of relocating collections to a new state-of-the-art storage facility six years ago, the Maine State Museum conducted an extensive review of nearly 100,000 items. During this process certain objects were determined inappropriate to the institution's mission. After careful analysis these were recommended for deaccession. The first disposal option was transfer to another museum. Where feasible the idea worked well. For instance, an unusual and rare Canadian railroad clock was given to an appropriate museum in Canada.

The Western Reserve Historical Society Museum in Cleveland carried out an inter-museum transfer two years ago. A wedding dress of little value to the institution's prominent costume collection was given to a local historical society. The dress has documentary importance for that organization and, indeed, had been on loan to it for nearly 10 years.

There will, of course, be times when inter-museum deaccessioning is not a viable option. It may prove difficult to locate an interested institution or one that will properly care for the collections being removed. Time might be a problem. Practical obstacles such as shipping may be difficult to overcome. Also, certain donor or other legal restrictions could require items be sold (or even destroyed) if they are unwanted.

The confusion sometimes surrounding deaccessioning cuts to the core of every museum's *raison d'être* and invariably manifests itself in the form of disturbing questions. Are museums public trust organizations? Should they honor implied agreements with previous, present, and future donors of objects, money, time, and other resources? Can museum beneficiaries truly believe these institutions? Are museums blatantly failing as preservation organizations? These questions and their answers are a mix of the highly charged, superficial, and complex. They have all arisen largely because of commercial deaccessioning.

Museums are hard pressed to avoid the extraordinary lure of the marketplace. The pressures to sell collections are enormous. Institutional budgets are always thin and income opportunities cannot be ignored. However, the immediate monetary benefits of selling may be offset by more devastating adverse long-term public relations effects.

Individually and collectively, museums must reconsider the viability of commercial deaccessioning as a first choice collection removal option. A museum's reputation is its most important asset. This is the foundation upon which success is built and maintained. Citizens have every right to demand that museums manage collections responsibly on their behalf. As preservation organizations first and foremost, museums need to consider the physical and intellectual well-being of what they deaccession. This may be best accomplished by inter-museum transfer.

Legacies and Heresies: Some Alternatives in Disposing of Museum Collections

By David W. Barr

W e've all seen it happen! The mere mention of removing any item, no matter how neglected, from a museum's collection is the surest way to arouse controversy, anguish and rage.

Deaccessioning and subsequent disposal of collections are among the most sensitive, yet unavoidable of routine museum professional responsibilities. This article is not fundamentally, however, about deaccessioning (since that is a matter for formal decision by each institution independently), but about how formally deaccessioned collections (or those that have never been accessioned) can safely be disposed of.

Makes it sound a little like disposing of hazardous chemicals doesn't it? And the analogy is not a bad one to keep in mind. Careless handling can threaten institutional health.

Once you get beyond the tough deaccessioning decision, simply getting rid of the object is not as simple as it may seem. Different types of collections carry different obligations and are surrounded by different sensitivities, especially for publicly supported institutions or those operating under some form of public mandate—for example, with charitable status for taxation purposes. Thus different proce-

David W. Barr served as curator, curatorial department head, and associate director at the Royal Ontario Museum, Toronto, Canada. He is now an independent museum consultant. "Legacies and Heresies: Some Alternatives in Disposing of Museum Collections" originally appeared in Muse, *volume VIII, no. 2, summer 1990, Ottawa: Canadian Museums Association (CMA). It is reprinted with the permission of both the CMA and the author.*

dures may be required, and making a mistake could bring both headaches and embarrassment to the institution.

PRUDENT BEGINNINGS

Just because disposal is so dangerous, it is well to preface any comments on alternatives with the prudent constraints on deciding to remove objects from collections held in public trust.

To begin with, the reason should be right. Objects should be removed only because they do not fit the approved collection mandate of the institution (because of past mistakes, revised mandates or continually increasing standards). The process should not be undertaken *solely* to make space, to raise money or for any other secondary reason.

Above all, before even considering deaccessioning, be sure your board has approved collection policies and procedures that specify how to proceed. Then, be sure you follow all approved policies and procedures scrupulously, obtaining board approval for each specific object removal when policy requires it. Any restrictions accepted from the original donor must be considered. Finally, make sure that you follow all applicable laws, for instance, those pertaining to Revenue Canada and The Cultural Property Import and Export Act. Consult a museum legal expert to be sure.

With the delicate matter of deaccessioning safely behind us, we're ready to examine the diversity of approaches that must be taken towards disposal. Although diversity is the key word, a few useful guidelines can serve to orient thinking for each of a range of different collection types. There is room here only to explore a few of the major variances that distinguish different collection materials.

FINE ARTS COLLECTIONS

Fine arts collections include those artifacts usually referred to as art: paintings, sculptures and drawings. Generally, the rationale for disposal of works of art is for collections improvement. That is, the "poorer" artifacts (in quality, taste, historic significance, representativeness, or authenticity) are sold to raise money to buy the "better." Occasionally disposal is done simply to weed out poorer material with no commercial value (same route but no requirement for monetary gain).

If money must be raised through the disposal, an appraisal should first be obtained so that any sale short of public auction will be deemed to have taken place at "market value." If the artifact was acquired through donation, the original donor or his/her descendants should be informed of the museum's intention, and they should be kept up to date on the progress if they request it. Next it is good practice to inquire within the institution, for another department (education, rentals, etc.) may have a valid use for the piece. If there are no takers from within, the responsibility of a public institution then demands that notice be circulated to other public institutions. But sibling institutions will be considered for transfer of title only if they offer to purchase at an appropriate price.

After these measures have been taken, and if no satisfactory buyer has been found, the next appropriate step is sale by public auction. Private sales should be avoided to prevent the appearance of favoritism. And of course, staff of the institution and members of its board can never receive deaccessioned artifacts or benefit personally from the transaction.

These days it is acceptable and probably desirable for the deaccessioning institution to be publicly identified at the time of the auction and in advance of advertising. Many institutions are uncomfortable with going public on the sale of former collections, but the practice ensures that there will be no appearance of hiding either the fact of the disposal or the identity of the buyer. And there is little danger of damaging public confidence in museums' custodial role as long as disposals are not wholesale.

Generally, disposal of donated material of commercial value that has not been accessioned is also carried out by proceeding to auction. This type of sale is really just the museum providing a service to the donor of converting the donation into cash, and has none of the implications of public accountability that apply to museum collections.

To preserve the maximum amount of information for unanticipated future uses, the history, attributes and circumstances of disposal of all deaccessioned collections should be thoroughly documented.

DECORATIVE ARTS

Decorative arts collections can be handled in the same manner as fine arts objects. Because the decorative arts can only be broadly defined, a museum must be watchful for the presence of artifacts of ritual and religious significance or those that represent the cultural heritage of any indigenous group of people. Such material may require special treatment.

Fine and decorative arts artifacts can serve as a model upon which disposal alternatives for other kinds of material may be seen as variations. For after leaving the relatively straightforward realms of the traditional arts, we enter an area of museum/gallery collections where there may exist special interest groups with claims beyond the public interest as normally defined. Here may be found different kinds of "property" that are not thought, in the best interests of society, to be appropriately held in private hands.

ETHNOGRAPHIC COLLECTIONS

Worldwide, museums have begun to recognize the legitimate interest that indigenous peoples may have in objects representing their own culture. At no time is this recognition more important than when one contemplates disposing of artifacts from an ethnographic collection. As noted above, first internal users and then sibling public institutions should be tried. Destruction is not an option for disposal of irreplaceable ethnographic collections, nor is sale for revenue generation. Among accredited public institutions, those run by native groups or devoted to exhibiting ethnographic collections should be given first consideration.

If no accredited institution can be identified, consideration should be given to transferring title to native organizations claiming an interest in the artifacts. Such a transfer of title should only be made, however, with satisfactory evidence of the ability to give responsible care and upon adequate indemnification by the recipients against claims from any additional interested groups that may later appear.

ARCHAEOLOGY COLLECTIONS

Archaeology collections can be treated according to the guidelines for ethnographic materials, with the additional simplification that the originating culture may be no longer extant. But there is also the additional complication that various countries may harbor claims to such artifacts as components of a historic national heritage.

If the deaccessioning institution has valid title to the artifacts, they should be offered for sale to the public institutions in the country of origin. But if the collections are found to have been acquired inadvertently in an illegal fashion, they should be returned forthwith to an appropriate official organization in the country of origin, where the capacity for responsible care can be demonstrated. If there is no other valid claimant, the strictures against public sale technically need not apply for archaeological materials, although many professional archaeologists are on record as opposing any commerce in such artifacts.

Faked archaeological artifacts discovered in a museum's collection present a special case. Forgeries can seldom be used to further understanding of the culture of interest. If no longer required for educational or research purposes, they may be offered for public sale immediately after deaccessioning. They should be ineradicably marked to prevent ever again being mistaken as authentic.

HISTORY COLLECTIONS

History collections, broadly defined, include the objects of everyday life, historic events, contemporary culture (ephemera, etc.) collections, instruments that illustrate the history of science and technology, stamps, coins and even historic sites and buildings. In this field occasional artifacts may be justly regarded as irreplaceable aspects of our heritage, and once sheltered under the umbrella of public institutional protections, can never again justifiably pass into private hands. When this is the case, the museum may have to consider itself "stuck" with the artifact or property in perpetuity if no other appropriate custodian can be found. Many years may have to be devoted to negotiating either with another custodian or with funding sources to enable the museum to care for the artifact or property appropriately.

Where there is no "unique" heritage aspect to these collections, standard disposal procedures for the fine and decorative arts can be applied.

Note that artifacts of unique "historic" significance may occur among all other kinds of collections and should be treated accordingly.

NATURAL HISTORY COLLECTIONS

In general, natural history collections are easier to deal with than artifacts since monetary values usually are not high, and biological specimens originate in natural populations that are, for the most part, self-regenerating. Disposal is normally by gift or destruction, seldom by sale. Nevertheless, environmental deterioration, international conventions on trade in endangered species and the loss of natural habitats have given a new significance to some natural history specimens.

First the simple cases. Specimens of the natural world (plants, animals, rocks and minerals) that represent samples from abundant sources are often collected solely for exchange or for "destructive" use in exhibitions or research, as well as for addition to the permanent research collections. Reciprocal exchange with other museum collections normally takes place without benefit of formal disposal "procedure." Annual notification of such exchanges should however, be made to museum management, with *pro forma* reporting to the board of trustees. Museums must always take care, however, that collecting for exchange or destructive purposes never becomes exploitative.

Specimens from the research collections may also be removed for (perhaps destructive) use in exhibitions or for destructive analysis in order to generate significant information. Specimens that are identified as surplus to research, exchange and exhibition needs, should first be offered to other public institutions before destruction is considered. And in all instances, responsible institutions in the country of origin of the collections should be given first consideration for deposit of the surplus material. Specimens found to have been inadvertently removed from the country of origin illegally should, of course, be returned forthwith.

There are, in addition, a variety of natural history specimens that must receive special treatment. *Types*, specimens that represent any of a variety of kinds of permanent standards, required again and again as scientific reference points, cannot be disposed of to other than another responsible custodial institution. The same is true of *voucher* specimens that represent permanent records of species identified in laboratory or environmental research. More formally, laws in many countries prohibit the transfer of bird and sometimes mammal specimens to other than approved institutions.

All specimens of rare, endangered or extinct species must also be preserved in a responsible public institution as irreplaceable documentation. Palaeontological collections may fall into any of these categories, but at the very least should be regarded as less replaceable than specimens from naturally regenerating living populations.

"Living" collections, such as those maintained by zoos and botanical gardens are no different than preserved specimens from natural populations and can be treated as noted above. Where the living specimen is representative of a rare or endangered species, the constraints of the public good are even more persuasive. And zoos should ensure that surplus animals sold privately are neither subjected to mistreatment nor hunted for a fee.

Protected lands and habitats, such as biological reserves share many of the characteristics of historic sites and buildings, and must be regarded as a permanent obligation of the responsible institutions, unless an appropriate surrogate can be identified.

COLLECTION SUPPORT MATERIAL

Collections documentation in the form of books, reprints, documents, tapes, photographs and the like do not normally fall under the formal collecting mandate of museums and galleries (although they may for libraries and archives). As a result, normal procedures for deaccessioning and disposal do not apply.

Nevertheless, with an increasing concern for the context and provenance of museum collections as an aspect of their significance and usefulness, responsible institutions would do well to adopt conservative practices for support material. Perhaps existing policies should be revised to reflect this new level of interest.

Especially if library donations have been made under the terms of the Cultural Property Import and Export Act, it would not hurt for any subsequent disposal to be made with benefit of full, board approved deaccessioning procedure.

POSTSCRIPT

Reflecting on this survey raises the question of just how professional museum workers are in the management of collections. Are the differences between collection practices for different materials really justified on the basis of historical circumstance? Or are there unrecognized commonalties that could not only unify a museological approach to collections but also require the revision of many existing special purpose policies?

Attitudes to Disposal from Museum Collections

By Geoffrey Lewis

For a paper[1] comparing attitudes to disposals from museum collections, the starting point would normally be an assessment of attitudes towards museum collecting itself. Examination of professional opinion and legal statements in governing legislation and elsewhere, however, reveals a surprising diversity of opinion. Further, there is at times a mis-match between the legislative perception of museums and their collections and actual practice: This can occur inconsistently within countries and there are certainly major variations between countries. From this it can be anticipated that a similar diversity of attitude exists towards disposal both between and within countries.

Before coming to the issues relating to the acquisition and disposal of museum collections, therefore, a brief examination of the notion of cultural property is desirable. This is the material of museum collections but it has its own independent legislation. How then have attitudes towards cultural property developed and what is their current standing? For the purposes of this article the term cultural property, following normal international practice, is taken to include material from the arts, humanities and sciences.[2]

Geoffrey Lewis has served as president of the U.K.'s Museums Association and president of the International Council of Museums. He currently sits on the editorial board of Museum Management and Curatorship. *"Attitudes to Disposal from Museum Collections" originally appeared in* Museum Management and Curatorship, *volume 11, 1992. It is reprinted with permission from Elsevier Science Ltd., Oxford, England.*

THE NOTION OF CULTURAL PROPERTY

Historical

The notion of the special nature of cultural property is of considerable antiquity. By the early 19th century it had already taken on a familiar form; for example, when the British Parliament considered the purchase of the Earl of Elgin's collection of marbles from the Parthenon, such issues as the propriety of ambassadorial collecting and the significance of a nation's cultural heritage were considered in the House of Commons (1816) debate. The restitution of the works of art which had been removed during the Napoleonic Wars, following the decision of the Congress of Vienna in 1815, is well known and another clear recognition of the special nature of cultural property at this time.

Much of the international recognition of the significance of cultural property occurs in legislation relating to its protection in the case of armed conflict. Thus, the Lieber Code, developed in 1863 for use during the American Civil War, allowed the appropriation of all public property by the victorious forces but required that works of art, libraries, collections, etc., should be protected and their eventual ownership determined by peace treaty. The Hague Convention of 1907 stated that "the property of institutions dedicated to educators, the arts and sciences, even when State property, shall be treated as private property." The Hague Convention of 1954,[3] currently in force, introduces a clear international aspect: "Cultural property belonging to any person whatsoever shall be recognized as the cultural heritage of all mankind." This is emphasized elsewhere in the Convention by suggesting that it is the "international responsibility of all nations to protect their own and other people's heritage."

In the 20 years from 1960 no fewer than 12 conventions or recommendations were passed by the UNESCO General Conference on the importance of cultural property; some of the reasons for this have been discussed elsewhere (Lewis, 1988). There has been similar activity at a regional level under the aegis of the Council of Europe, commencing with the European Cultural Convention of 1954 from which developed, in due course, conventions on the archaeological and architectural heritage, with the most recent, in 1985, covering offenses concerned with cultural property. For that matter the Treaty of Rome—

concerned as it is with establishing a common market and therefore the free flow of trade within the European Communities—has a specific clause in it to allow restrictions on the movement of art objects with a view to protecting national treasures of an artistic, historic or archaeological value.[4]

Contemporary Legal Attitudes to Cultural Property

At an international level, attention must be drawn particularly to the UNESCO Convention of 1970[5] which today continues to provide an important statement on the international attitude towards cultural property. It is interesting, from a European standpoint, to compare the region's approach to this UNESCO legislation with that of the European Convention on the archaeological heritage, passed by the Council of Europe in 1969.[6] Both are concerned with counteracting illicit transfers between countries as a safeguard to the heritage of the country of origin and particularly the scientific integrity of the material. Sixteen European states,[7] including the United Kingdom, have ratified the legislation on the archaeological heritage, but only five member states of the Council of Europe[8] have endorsed UNESCO's 1970 Convention. Britain is not among them.

North America

The notion of cultural property as applied to the United States heritage is not recognized in export law in that country. Indeed there are no restrictions, other than for archaeological material, on the export of cultural property. It should, however, be noted that the United States does have cultural property legislation in relation to the import of heritage material from other nations.[9] In this aspect it ratifies the 1970 UNESCO Convention on illicit trafficking. As Malaro (1985) points out, however, it was not the intention of the U.S. Congress in enacting this legislation to control museum acquisition policies, and it was left to museums to conform voluntarily to the standards set in the legislation; many have done so.

Canada passed cultural property protective legislation in 1975;[10] in doing so it ratified the 1970 UNESCO Convention and was one of the first industrialized nations to do so. In drawing this up certain assumptions were allowed:

■ that important aspects of the Canadian heritage should be kept in the country;

■ that those owning such material should not be penalized simply because they wished to sell it abroad or otherwise export it;

■ that the system of control should be voluntary, but actively supported by the relevant private, commercial and custodial communities;

■ that because of the voluntary nature of legal compliance, substantial incentives for those affected by it had to be provided;

■ the importation of cultural property into Canada should be in such a way as to respect the laws of other countries (Cameron, 1980).

This legislation can be regarded as closer in spirit to the UNESCO 1970 Convention than that for the U.S.A.

Europe

Apart from England and the Republic of Ireland, civil law systems prevail in the countries of Western Europe under which public property is normally regarded as inalienable in the law of the public domain. Thus, the inclusion of public museums within the terms of public domain legislation provides very strong protection for state museum collections. This is the position in France[11] where the principle has been extended to local government and other public bodies,[12] thus preventing disposal also from the collections held by these museums. This means that only material in private museums and collections does not have this protection, although important works in private hands are classified,[13] preventing export. Powers to declassify inalienable material in France have never been extended to cultural goods.

Similar principles apply in Italy,[14] Spain and Switzerland. In Spain the legislation, with its concept of inalienability, has been developed to include all archaeological discoveries,[15] as well as the property of the Royal Crown.[16] Cultural property in the possession of religious institutions also is closely controlled and may be transferred only to the state, other public bodies or to other religious institutions.[17] Different circumstances prevail in Belgium where ecclesiastical material is considered part of the public domain together with certain monuments, edifices and their contents. However, other cultural property, such as that in public museums, is not classified in this way in Belgium.[18]

Specific cultural property legislation applies in a number of European countries, whether or not they operate under a civil code. The form of this legislation varies considerably. It can relate to the whole artistic, historic and scientific heritage or only to a narrow subject area within one of these fields; it may be concerned with all heritage material or only with specified material of excellence within it; it may relate to named material only. In addition, different principles may be applied to different types of owner or be invoked only in a certain set of circumstances, such as export or death.

A number of European countries have general, cultural property legislation which protects the artistic and historic heritage and in some cases extends to the natural sciences. In the case of Greece, however, the legislation[19] is specific and protects the excavated archaeological heritage and works of art made prior to 1830. In Sweden and the United Kingdom, legal protection of cultural property applies only in the event of export. Treasure Trove, a common law inheritance in England, may contribute protection in certain cases but it is not, of course, cultural property legislation. Taxation relief in respect of the transfer of heritage material to the public sector in the United Kingdom (Lewis, 1990) may also be regarded as a protective measure where a museum is the beneficiary.

Those countries with general protective legislation will normally classify the material concerned, and this presupposes some form of listing or registration. The arrangements for designating cultural property are normally organized at a national level, but in Germany and Switzerland this is the responsibility of the Länder and Cantons, respectively, while in Belgium[20] the matter of cultural objects may be dealt with at community level. The administration of the schemes falls under a variety of government offices and not necessarily the government department which has responsibility for museums.

Other Countries

Cultural property legislation in many countries reveals the harsh truth that a scarce commodity or a denuded heritage will concentrate the mind in this matter. The impetus for, and subsequent ratifications of, the 1970 UNESCO Convention on illicit trafficking came mainly from the non-industrialized countries. In Africa, the Arab world and, to a considerable extent, Asia and Latin America, cultural property legislation claims all such material to the state and may prohibit its disposal and export or at least require government approval before any transfer can take place (i.e., Algeria, Angola, Jordan, Kenya). Sometimes the law will allow for pre-emption by the state concerned (i.e., Israel, Kuwait, Libya, Nicaragua, to name a few countries that take this view). There can be no doubt of the special character of cultural property and, with few exceptions, notably the United States of America, countries go to considerable lengths to protect this aspect of their heritage. This is the material that museums collect, and the question now is whether these concepts are reflected in the museum legislation.

LEGAL ATTITUDES TO MUSEUM COLLECTIONS

In view of the extensive legislation covering cultural property, it might be expected that the primacy of the collection and its protection would be to the fore in museum and related legislation. In fact this is by no means always the case. Museum-enabling legislation, where it exists, is often more concerned with the utilization of the collection. This may be perfectly acceptable where there is separate strong legislation protecting cultural property, but otherwise it fails to address that tension between preservation and use which is so prominent in museum work. As a result, considerable variations of emphasis on objectives occur which may substantially affect attitudes both to collection and disposal.

United States

The majority of United States museums are outside the public sector, operating as nonprofit organizations, and can often be classified as charitable corporations. There is no law governing the museums of the United States *per se* and therefore no federal or state requirement on such institutions other than those that apply to all such bodies. The legal position of the United States' nonprofit organizations is that they have powers to dispose of their assets—collections being viewed as realizable assets—unless their charters specifically limits this. The approach to deaccessioning amongst the country's museums results, therefore, from local determination by the museums' own governing bodies.

In expressing an American viewpoint, therefore, Marie Malaro (1985) states that collecting is a "combination of intelligent selection and thoughtful pruning." In this she follows closely the ruling in the Wilstach Estate[21] case where despite requirements by Will for the collection of Mrs. Wilstach "to be preserved . . . taken care of . . . kept in good order . . . kept together," it was determined that as the collection had been provided "as a nucleus or foundation of an Art Gallery for the use and enjoyment of the people," buying and selling was a necessary power to exercise this properly. This is of course only one case but the precedent could be developed, for example, in the case of a collection given for educational purposes. This could reduce a museum collection to little more than an educational resource centre whose holdings should change at the whim and fancy of educational fashion.

Another factor appears to have affected United States' attitudes. A number of its museums developed initially out of the desire to diffuse knowledge and refine public taste rather than to house an existing collection. This brings different requirements from, for example, the responsibility of a scholarly collection in a museum's formative years. In the latter case its significance and permanence as an archive is likely to be emphasized, although there is a variety of approaches in the different disciplines, as Marie Malaro (1985) points out. These differences, of course, relate to purpose. Art collections tend to be made to be viewed. The finds from a scientifically conducted archaeological excavation, however, may never be shown but are no less important as an historical document. For zoological and botanical material, of course, the same may well apply in addition to its significance as a taxonomic or habitat archive.

Europe

In Europe there is a strong presumption against disposal, in contrast to the circumstances and practice in the United States.[22] This is no doubt influenced partly by the Roman legal tradition where public domain legislation prevents disposal from museum collections in certain countries. However, the general tenor of national museum legislation, where it exists, is against transfers from collections and then, if this occurs, only between museums. The trustees of the national museums in Britain, *inter alia*, are required to care for, preserve and add to the objects in their collections; they are empowered to dispose of items only if they are duplicates, are unsuitable to be retained in the collection (having regard to student usage) or have become unsuitable by reason of damage or deterioration. A very restrictive definition of the word "duplicate" is applied. The National Gallery, however, has been prevented by statute from disposing of any of its collections since 1954. The transfer of items between certain national museums is authorized under the same legislation.[23]

The legal position of the non-national museums of Europe is less clear, although the same principles appear customarily to be followed in the public sector. Where transfers occur, they will be only on the decision of the governing board of the museum; a gift with conditions may require higher authorization.

In some cases, museums do not have separate legal identify from the government that established them or authorized their existence. Other countries, however, appear to be giving their national museums greater autonomy. In Spain, the Prado now has separate legal identity[24] with stronger powers than other museums in Spain; these prevent the sale or exchange of works of art from its collection. The Centro de Arte Reina Sofia in Madrid has similar status.

This is also the case in the United Kingdom, and greater autonomy and powers have been given to a number of the national museums over the last 10 years: the Victoria and Albert Museum, the National Museum of Science and Industry (the Science Museum), the Royal Armouries[25] and the Royal Museums of Scotland[26] are all now governed by statute. In comparison, recent museum legislation in Britain gives a clearer statement of the museum function and therefore of the duties of trustees. However, there is still considerable imprecision in much of the extant legislation regarding the full objectives of a museum. They have no legal mandate, *per se*, to ensure the collection and protection of the nation's moveable cultural property. This is not peculiar to the United Kingdom.[27] In Austria[28] and France, for example, the notion of a "museum"—which, as in the United Kingdom, may be a private or public-sector institution—does not find expression in museum legislation.

It might be argued that recent national museum legislation in Britain under National Heritage Acts[29] implies that they are the repository for the nation's cultural heritage. However, this concept normally comes into its own only where the museum legislation is integral with that for the protection of an aspect of the cultural heritage. This is the case in Poland[30] and also in Greece[31] where all excavated archaeological material and works of art made prior to 1830 are protected.

However, there is some evidence of changing attitudes in certain countries of Europe. In Britain the government department concerned with museums, the Office of Arts and Libraries, undertook in 1989 a study on the disposal of museum collections,[32] although the outcome of this has still to be announced. In February 1991 the Audit Commission (1991) reported on their "value for money study" of local government museums and galleries in England and Wales[33] and recommended that government should clarify the law regarding the disposal of museum collections. In Sweden a new policy was introduced in the state budget for 1990-91, which announced that items "useless and not required for the activities of the museum" may be sold.[34] The National Swiss Museum has authority to sell works of art from its collection, provided two similar works remain, or if they are surplus to requirements.[35] However, the constitutions of a number of Swiss private museums prohibit sales from their collections.

Other Countries

As already noted above, a number of the national museums in African and Middle Eastern states operate under antiquities legislation and serve as the national repository for archaeological material. Perhaps one of the most comprehensive of these is in Nigeria.[36] Here the National Commission for Museums and Monuments has responsibilities for the control of all antiquities, ethnology, science and technology, as well as natural history material within the country, and provides national museums in most of the component states. This service provides a national repository for the country's cultural property. The National

Museum in Wellington, New Zealand, also has a specific mandate to act as a national repository for New Zealand material generally.[37]

PROFESSIONAL ATTITUDES

Illicit trade (moral and legal considerations apart) suppresses information to the detriment of scholarship and the understanding of the specimen. The International Council of Museums (ICOM) issued a statement on the ethics of acquisition at the time of the 1970 UNESCO Convention but this has now been superseded by a much fuller statement in its *Code of Professional Ethics* (ICOM, 1990). This code suggests *inter alia* that each museum authority should publish, and regularly review, its collecting policy; ensure that it acquires valid title to all acquisitions; respect wildlife protection and conservation legislation in collecting for the natural sciences; and refuse to purchase material illicitly removed from archaeological sites. There is a general presumption of the permanence of museum collections, that in the event of disposal other museums should have first refusal and that any moneys resulting from a sale should be used solely to supplement the collections. In the event of a request for the return of cultural property to its country of origin, dialogue based on scientific and professional principles should be initiated between the parties.

Ethical codes and guidelines on museum collections have been drawn up in a number of countries and they generally emphasize the permanent nature of museums and their collections. In addition, some museums have their own statements; an example is that of the Royal Ontario Museum in Toronto.[38] This code states that collections will maintain their significance only as long as the individual objects retain their physical integrity, authenticity and usefulness for public and research purposes. Selective disposals are considered acceptable where objects no longer have one or more of these attributes. In making this statement the code also states that the museum fully recognizes its role as guardian of public property.

In the absence of ratification of the 1970 UNESCO Convention by the governments of some of the major nations in Europe, the museum profession has paid particular attention to codifying its position in the matter. In the United Kingdom, for example, the British Museum, the Museums Association and other national bodies issued a statement[39] as early as 1972 clarifying their position in the matter; this statement is endorsed in subsequent policy statements by the Museums Association, including its *Code of Conduct for Museum Curators*.[40]

SOME CONCLUSIONS

The extent and nature of the international legislation on cultural property provides a clear indication of its international and national importance. The notions which have been associated with it over the last two centuries help to identify its special significance. It is a special class of property, and society considers that it needs to be protected. Further, although it may be publicly owned, it is to be treated separately from public property. It is viewed, simultaneously, as the "cultural heritage of all mankind" and also as a means of promoting national identity. The latter has a particular bearing on disposal, the issues concerning the prohibition of illicit transfers of cultural property and, for that mater, on requests from nations for the return or restitution of material.

At the same time this body of international legislation also recognizes the scientific value of the material—including the site or context from which it may be derived and that much of it is the primary evidence contributing information and understanding to different disciplines. Its contributions to knowledge and its ability to promote cultural understanding together make it an important medium for exhibition, education and entertainment. Because of these factors there has to be close control on transfers of ownership of important cultural property internationally, regionally and nationally.

At the operational level among the nations of Europe, there appears to be strong support for the protection of the archaeological heritage which is paralleled by that for the natural heritage. This is not reflected, however, in recognition of the broader protection of cultural property which could be offered through ratifying the 1970 UNESCO Convention. The national legislation in Europe, with the possible exception of Switzerland and Sweden, does provide some protection but is diverse in character and varying in the protection it affords. Those countries operating with public domain legislation provide stronger protection—inalienability—to cultural property in national collections. Some countries may provide supplementary legislation to meet particular requirements. There are, however, certain disadvantages, one of which is the generality of a code for public property and the lack of flexibility that this brings when the special requirements of cultural property, such as temporary export for exhibition purposes, have to be met.

Legislation governing the administration of museums and their collections is normally subsidiary to national laws governing cultural property. These national provisions are, however, fragmented and unclear, particularly among the industrialized nations. A key problem appears to be the failure to link the notion of a nation's heritage with museum collections. As a result the emphasis may centre on collection utilization rather than protection, and at worst may see the collection only as an exploitable resource. There is a case for model legislation to be drawn up by representatives of all interested parties which takes a comprehensive view of the museum function.

That model should give pre-eminence to the character of museum collections as a part of the nation's heritage, but it must recognize the need for collection control with rational decision-making both in the collection and disposal of specimens. The policy for this should be based on informed opinion from all interests represented in museum collections. Criteria to achieve this need to be established, but in the United Kingdom some important first indicators are available in the guidelines for the registration of museums. It would be necessary, however, to go much further than these, including the establishment of more specific criteria in relation to different types of collection. The matter is urgent and professional initiative should be encouraged rather than leaving the matter to uninformed legislators.

Acknowledgments

I would particularly acknowledge my gratitude to Marie Malaro whose paper[41] stimulated thought in new directions, which is reflected here, and to the Museums Association for inviting me to contribute to their seminar on this topic. Certain of the information in this paper was gathered by the organizers of the "Third Symposium on the International Art Trade and Law," held in Amsterdam in June 1990 and analysed and presented there by the author (Lewis, 1991). This opportunity is also gratefully acknowledged.

Notes

1. The substance of this paper was given at the Museums Association seminar "Disposals from Museum Collections" at the Museum of London, 18 February 1991, and was in part a commentary on a paper by Marie C. Malaro prepared for the seminar but in the event not delivered (published in *Museum Management and Curatorship*, 10(3), September 1991, pp. 273-279).

2. See, for example, the definition in the UNESCO Convention on the means of prohibiting and preventing the illicit import, export and transfer of ownership of cultural property, 1970. The term cultural property is the subject of some dissatisfaction because of the connotation of commercial exploitability. O'Keefe and Prott (1989) prefer the term "cultural heritage."

3. UNESCO, Final Act of the Intergovernmental Conference on the Protection of Cultural Property in the Event of Armed Conflict, The Hague, 1954.

4. European Communities, Treaty of Rome, 1957; Article 36.

5. UNESCO—Convention on the Means of Prohibiting and Preventing the Illicit Import, Export and Transfer of Ownership of Cultural Property, 1970.

6. Council of Europe, European Convention on the Protection of the Archaeological Heritage, 1969.

7. Austria, Belgium, Denmark, France, Germany, Greece, Italy, Liechtenstein, Luxembourg, Malta, Portugal, Spain, Sweden, Switzerland and the United Kingdom.

8. Cyprus, Greece, Italy, Portugal and Spain.

9. United States, Convention on Cultural Property Implementation Act, 1983.

10. Canada, Cultural Property Export and Import Act 1975.

11. France, Code on the Public Domain, article 52.

12. France, Law 88-13 of January 1988, article 13.1.

13. France, Law of 31 December 1913.

14. Italy, Royal Decree 363 of 30 January 1913 and Law 1089/39 of 1 June 1939.

15. Spain, Law on Historical Patrimony 1985, article 44.

16. Spain, Law on National Patrimony 1982, article 6.2.

17. Spain, Law on Historical Patrimony 1985, article 28.2.

18. Belgium, La Cour de Cassation, 11 November 1886, pas, 1886, 1, p. 410.

19. Greece, Antiquities Law: 5351 of 1932.

20. Belgium, Flemish Decree of 17 November 1982.

21. Court advice given to the trustees of the W. P. Wilstach collection in 1954. The collection was donated originally to the city of Philadelphia.

22. See Malaro (1985, 1991) and Weil (1990), for example.

23. United Kingdom, National Gallery and Tate Gallery Act, 1954.

24. Spain, Royal Decree 1432/1985.

25. United Kingdom, National Heritage Act 1983.

26. United Kingdom, National Heritage (Scotland) Act, 1985.

27. United Kingdom, Inheritance Tax Act, 1984, schedule 3, describes a museum—in the specialized context of taxation relief—as "any institution which exists wholly or mainly for the purpose of preserving for the public benefit a collection of scientific, historic or artistic interest."

28. Austria, Federal Law of 1 July 1981 on the organization of research. This describes the tasks of museums as: collecting, safeguarding, presenting to the public and inventorying art objects, undertaking research and advising other museums (Bundesgesetzblatt, 1989: 663).

29. United Kingdom, National Heritage Act, 1983; National Heritage (Scotland) Act, 1985; for example.

30. Poland, Law on the Protection of Cultural Property and on Museums, 15 February 1962, Article 46.

31. Greece, Antiquities Law 5351 of 1932.

32. United Kingdom, "Powers of Disposal from Museum and Gallery Collections: a consultative paper," issued by the Office of Arts and Libraries, August 1988 (typewritten report).

33. United Kingdom, "The Road to Wigan Pier?: Managing Local Authority Museums and Galleries," Audit Commission for Local Authorities and the National Health Service in England and Wales (HMSO, London, 1991).

34. Sweden, State Budget, 1990-91.

35. Switzerland, Federal Law of 27 June 1890: The Swiss National Museum.

36. Nigeria, Decree 77 of 28 September 1979: The National Commission for Museums and Monuments Decree 1979.

37. New Zealand, National Art Gallery, Museum and War Memorial Act, 1972, Section 11.

38. Royal Ontario Museum, "Statement of Principles and Policies on Ethics and Conduct," Toronto, 1982.

39. The statement included the following: "That it is and will continue to be the practice of museums and galleries in the United Kingdom that they do not and will not knowingly acquire any antiquities or other cultural material which they have reason to believe has been exported in contravention of the current laws of the country of origin."

40. See also Malaro (1991) for the new code of ethics adopted in the U.S.A.

41. Op. cit., note 1.

References

Audit Commission (1991). "The Road to Wigan Pier?: Managing Local Authority Museums and Art Galleries." London: HMSO.

Cameron, Duncan (1980). *An Introduction to the Cultural Property Export and Import Act*, Arts and Culture Branch, Department of Communications, Government of Canada.

International Council of Museums (1970). *Ethics of Acquisition.* Paris: ICOM.

International Council of Museums (1990). *Statutes [&] Code of Professional Ethics.* Paris: ICOM.

Lewis, Geoffrey (1981). "The Return of Cultural Property," *Journal of the Royal Society of Arts*, 129: 435-443.

Lewis, Geoffrey (1988). "Museums: International and National Self-regulation," in P. Lalive (ed.) *International Sales of Works of Art*, pp. 557-565. Paris: ICC and University of Geneva.

Lewis Geoffrey (1990). "Heritage Giving through Taxation in the United Kingdom," in P. Lalive (ed.) *International Sales of Works of Art*, Volume 2. Paris: ICC Publishing; Deventer: Kluwer.

Lewis, Geoffrey (1991). "International Issues Concerning Museum Collections," in M. Briat and J. A. Freedberg (eds.) *International Sales of Works of Art*, Volume 3. Paris: ICC Publishing; Deventer: Kluwer.

Malaro, Marie (1985). *A Legal Primer on Managing Museum Collections.* Washington, D.C.: Smithsonian Institution Press.

Malaro, Marie (1991). "Deaccessioning: The American Perspective," *Museum Management and Curatorship*, 10 (3): 273-279.

O'Keefe, P. J. and Prott, L. V. (1989). *Law and Cultural Heritage. Volume 3: Movement.* London: Butterworths.

Weil, Stephen E. (1990). *Rethinking the Museum and Other Meditations.* Washington, D.C.: Smithsonian Institution Press.

The Deaccessioning Strategy at Glenbow, 1992-97

By Patricia Ainslie

INTRODUCTION

I n 1993, Glenbow adopted several strategies to ensure that the museum would continue to thrive in the future. We have structured our organization and are streamlining our work processes in response to reductions in income from both public and private sources. In addition, we have renewed our commitment to public service and are developing commercial ventures through Glenbow Enterprises to generate more revenue. As part of this work, we are refining our international collections. After the first two decades of worldwide collecting, Glenbow has increasingly focused its mandate, with a primary emphasis on the history and settlements of northwestern North America. This current deaccessioning[1] strategy involves focusing more closely on this core mandate. Glenbow will deaccession and sell selected items from its international collections in order to create a Collections Endowment Fund. This fund will be protected against inflation and kept intact for the future building of the collections. The income from this endowment will be dedicated to the care and maintenance of the core collections.

Early in June 1992, Glenbow's senior management team reviewed a five-year budget forecast. All of our revenues from the public and private sector were decreasing, but we were not sure what were the long-term implications. The shocking news was that at the current

Patricia Ainslie is director of collections at Glenbow, Calgary, Alberta, Canada. "The Deaccessioning Strategy at Glenbow, 1992-97" originally appeared in Museum Management and Curatorship, *volume 15, 1996. It is reprinted with permission from Elsevier Science Ltd., Oxford, England.*

rate of expenditure we would be bankrupt in five years, with an accumulated deficit of $7.7 million. Recognizing that one of our fiduciary
responsibilities is to ensure the continuity of the museum for the community, this situation created a need for immediate action. In late June
we spent a weekend off site to plan. We developed many ideas which
were refined to six strategies intended to guide us into a healthy future.
It was in this context that deaccessioning, one of the six strategies, was
seen as a way to augment income to care for collections, while at the
same time refining and focusing our collections. We felt that deaccessioning was a prudent, responsible and realistic approach given our
current situation and the nature of our collections.

Glenbow is the largest museum in Western Canada, with a collection of approximately 1.2 million objects and three floors of exhibition space totalling over 93,000 square feet. The diverse collections
include the disciplines of art, cultural history, military history, ethnology and mineralogy, consisting of 240,000 objects. In addition, Glenbow has the largest library of Western Canadiana and the largest non-
government archives in Canada. Glenbow's primary mandate is to document and preserve the history and development of the northwest
quadrant of North America, and secondly, to provide a national and international context for these core collections. However, Glenbow is unique
in Canada due to our history and the way in which some of our collections were acquired. Eric L. Harvie, Glenbow's founder, was a phil-
anthropist with eclectic tastes and wide-ranging interests. He built two
major collections: the Glenbow Collection of over 120,000 objects, plus
books, archives and photographs, which was given to the people of
Alberta in 1966, and the Riveredge Collection of over 37,000 objects,
plus books, archives and photographs, gathered from 1966 to 1979,
when it was given to the Province of Alberta. Glenbow holds both of
these collections in trust. Over the years, other donations and purchases have been added to these collections.

As Harvie collected art and artifacts from Canada and around the
world, he did so with the passion and enthusiasm of a collector in the
true Victorian sense of the word, and not always with the professional eye of a curator. He told his staff to go out and, "Collect like a bunch
of drunken sailors."[2] As the collections grew, new warehouses were

found to house them. One of Harvie's more intriguing enterprises was the acquisition of entire private collections or major holdings from museums. In 1964, over 600 objects were purchased from the Royal United Services Museum in London. These now form the core of Glenbow's military collection. The Schuller Museum of Art and Chivalry in New Hampshire was acquired in 1973 and included medieval arms and armour, Japanese armour and saddles, and European 16th-, 17th- and 18th-century furniture. To augment the Native American collections, Harvie bought the Roe Indian Museum from Pipestone, Minn.; the Sioux Indian Museum from Sioux Falls, S.D.; and the Fort Cherokee Indian Museum from Oklahoma. For the Canadiana collection, Harvie acquired the Frontier Ghost Town, a carnival and museum with over 6,000 items, mostly from old mining towns in British Columbia. As a result of these large-scale purchases, the quality of the collections is uneven. Certain collections have outstanding range and depth, while others lack cohesion, focus and relevance to Glenbow's mandate. In the early years, some entire collections were transferred to other institutions, as exemplified by the archaeology collection which was transferred to the University of Calgary.

The Glenbow-Alberta Institute was established 15 April 1966, through an act passed by the Alberta legislature. The departments of cultural and military history, ethnology, art, mineralogy, library and archives were amalgamated, and the collections were housed under one roof beginning in 1976 when Glenbow moved to its Ninth Avenue S.E. location in Calgary. Two years later, in May 1978, Glenbow developed a policy for deaccessioning, and this policy has been updated over the years. Deaccessioning became an active part of professional collections management at Glenbow through the 1980s. Collections care involves maintenance and ongoing expense, and we can no longer justify retaining material which is not germane to our purposes. In the 1980s, objects were deaccessioned primarily because they were reproductions, were not of museum quality, were duplicates inferior to material remaining in the collection, or lacked provenance. Most of this deaccessioned material was sold at auction in Calgary and the proceeds were put into an acquisition fund. Up to 1992 and the beginning of the current Deaccessioning Strategy, we had deaccessioned 18,056 items from the Glenbow Collection and 12,491 items from the Riveredge Collection.

The current plan will allow us to continue to refine parts of the collections not central to our mandate, as well as to raise funds for the preservation and future stability of the collections. It will allow Glenbow to define more closely its mandate regarding the international collections and to focus these collections more clearly, but we will remain committed to keeping selected international collections. It is with this current Deaccessioning Strategy that we depart from tradition. We planned to deaccession collections of high value and of museum quality, but which we felt were outside our core purposes. We also planned to expand the use of funds earned from the sale of nine collections to allow us to use the income generated by the Collections Endowment Fund for care and maintenance of the collections. This involves:

- conservation and preservation,
- registration,
- documentation and cataloguing,
- storage,
- research of objects, and
- acquisition of new material.

This also includes salaries of staff dedicated to the above activities. Excluded are exhibitions, programming and publications, and all other activities not directly related to the care of the collections. The central principle in this Deaccessioning Strategy was that Glenbow's curatorial staff would make the selection based on their knowledge of the collection and their field. The process for all deaccessioning involves selection of material by the curator responsible for the collection, approval by the director of collections and by the executive director, then recommendation for approval by the Collections Management Committee, and approval by the board of governors. There are clear policies, procedures, and a system of checks and balances to guide Glenbow's deaccessioning.

We knew it was essential to base our project on thorough research and planning, and consequently studied the literature relating to deaccessioning in Canada, the United States and the United Kingdom. There were certainly enough articles on the pitfalls! Our research was aided by the excellent articles published in *Muse* in 1990 by Elaine Tolmatch, registrar at the Montreal Museum of Fine Arts, which included a "Checklist of Considerations for Formulating a Deaccession and Disposal Policy,"[3] and a bibliography.[4] Though deaccessioning is not considered common practice in Canada, various museums have deaccessioned some material. In a recent survey of 14 museums and art galleries, including six of the largest in Canada, all but two had deaccessioned between two and 400 items over the past 10 to 20 years. The reasons for deaccessioning included, lack of provenance or data, poor condition, duplication, outside of mandate, and not legally owned. Only two museums had deaccessioned over 400 items, and one over 1,000. The latter had deaccessioned over 30,000 objects, due primarily to repository changes of archaeological material which was transferred, some of which was repatriated, as well as the destruction of degraded scientific specimens once research experiments were complete. Only four of these museums had sold some of the material deaccessioned. All but one had a policy or criteria and procedures for deaccessioning.

Only two examples of Canadian museum deaccessioning have to date been publicly documented—the Western Development Museum (WDM) and the New Brunswick Museum. The WDM provides a good model of careful planning and execution of a complex and extensive deaccessioining project undertaken in the mid 1980s. Objects deaccessioned were given to other nonprofit museums in Saskatchewan, and the remaining material was sold at public auction, while the moneys realized were to be used for acquisition, cataloguing, conservation and restoration. Due to careful planning and consultation, there was no negative response to this deaccessioning.[5] On the other hand, the deaccessioning of over 700 objects at the New Brunswick Museum led to a public outcry and a government enquiry. Lack of adequate planning and consultation can have disastrous results.[6]

THE DEACCESSIONING PROCESS

While research was ongoing, we completed the Terms of Reference for our project in late July 1992, with the following purposes:

- ■ To sell selected collections or items from the international collections, including high value items;

■ To create a Collections Endowment Fund, indexed against inflation, and to use the income for the care and maintenance of the collections at Glenbow and for future acquisitions;

■ To create space for new acquisitions of more relevant collections;

■ To focus more clearly the collections, remove some international collections, and establish renewed focus on our core mandate of northwestern North America;

■ To rationalize and reduce collections by culling duplicates, non-museum quality items; and

■ To reduce the cost of collections management.

Late in July 1992, a team was selected which consisted of Daryl Betenia (chief registrar), Gerald Conaty (curator of ethnology), Barry Agnew (curator of military history), Frances Roback (assistant curator of cultural history), Len Gottselig (chief librarian) and Jackie Eliasson (acquisitions coordinator). As the chief curator, the present author served as project team leader, and performed the role of curator of art.

Our first team meeting was held 4 August 1992, and it was immediately clear that the first major challenge would be to win curatorial support for this strategic initiative. There was resistance to the project for several reasons, including moral and ethical concerns, the proposed loss of some international collections, and the broader use of funds from deaccessioning. Until we had an open and thorough airing of these issues, we could not proceed effectively. We therefore planned a meeting for 10 September 1992 to include our team, a cross-section of Glenbow staff, the executive director, and members of Glenbow's board of governors. The team developed the questions for what was to be a lengthy meeting with substantial debate. The seven questions were:

1. Should an object be kept in the public domain for public benefit or should the object be sold for the highest price in order to increase the museum's own assets?

2. In the light of the "Task Force Report on Museums and First Peoples" prepared by the Assembly of First Nations and the Canadian Museums Association (1992), which recommended that we consider current moral rather than past legal standards for acqui-

sitions, how do we deal with objects and collections we would consider unethical to acquire today?

3. Should we deaccession international collections which are of national significance and which make Glenbow unique?, i.e., international firearms, American illustrator art.

4. Should proceeds be applied to acquisitions, storage, conservation, or operating expenses?

5. Is public auction preferable to private sale?

6. Should we exclude donations due to donor sensitivity?

7. Will the public perceive that the deaccessioning and disposal program promotes the museum's purposes and goals? Will the public perceive deaccessioning to be in its best interests?

The result of the discussion was a fair degree of consensus on the way to proceed. It was agreed that public institutions in Canada would be given a reasonable opportunity to purchase objects, but not at the expense of the efficiency or effectiveness of the process. They would be expected to pay a fair market price and negotiations would not be allowed to drag on unduly. We would carefully consider the rationale for deaccessioning each collection and, with each, address any of the possible ethical issues. We decided to keep objects which were too sensitive, such as the Kachina dolls from the ethnographic collection from the southwestern United States. Kachinas, dolls for teaching important lessons to children, have been sold commercially, but since they are now considered religious by certain people, some museums are restricting access to them to avoid controversy. We decided not to deaccession them.

There was agreement that we must focus the collections and make appropriate decisions in *each* collection area without applying any kind of blanket deaccessioning policy. There was consensus that only *income* from moneys raised would be used for the direct care and maintenance of the collections and that this should be strictly defined. There was agreement that material would be sold in the manner most appropriate to the specific collection. Auction would be preferable to private sale as it is the most public method. We decided that for donated items, we would approach donors and obtain their agreement to any proposed deaccessioning. In fact, when we reviewed the collections, there were very few privately donated objects, and we decided to exclude them altogether. Most of the 3,000 items that were subsequently selected were from the Glenbow Collection, the major public gift made by Eric Harvie to the people of Alberta in 1966. Not more than 20 other items, purchased after 1966, were deaccessioned. We also realized that if the process was to be credible, the whole deaccessioning program would have to be communicated very carefully and clearly to the public. We had to be prepared to deal with adverse public reaction if it materialized. As a result, we decided that Glenbow's name would be used in the sale of all deaccessioned objects. Overall, it was acknowledged that deaccessioning was a healthy practice for Glenbow; it had been important through the 1980s to focus our collections and this current Deaccessioning Strategy was necessary to guarantee the future care of the collections. This special meeting and the ongoing team meetings built support for the process among staff, while one of the first things we did was to draft a preliminary communications statement, in case the news of our deaccessioning activity became known before we were ready. It was important to us that the public understood what we were doing and why, and as the work progressed this statement was refined.

GOING PUBLIC

During October and November 1992, each member of the team contacted professional colleagues to discuss our deaccessioning project and to seek their comments and input. We were surprised at the level of support from most colleagues, although there were cautionary comments— all of which we considered as we proceeded. We talked to some major donors and, when they understood the background, they were supportive of our strategy. We met with our founder's son, Donald Harvie, who was at that time a member of our Collections Management Committee and our board of governors. We knew that most of the items proposed for deaccessioning would come from his father's collections. Donald Harvie was supportive in principle, but wanted to approve each step of the process and each listed collection. We also had discussions with our partners, the City of Calgary and the provincial government, as well as the Canadian Museums Association (CMA) and the Canadian Cultural Property Export Review Board (CCPERB).

Robert R. Janes, the executive director of Glenbow, presented our six guiding operational strategies to the Canadian Museum Directors Group (CMDG) and the Canadian Art Museum Directors Organization (CAMDO). The museum directors were concerned about the deaccessioning, but felt Glenbow was in a unique position due to the size, value and overall diversity of the collections. CAMDO, while it acknowledged that Glenbow must plan for its own future and complimented us on our open communication, was nevertheless cautionary with some members openly opposed. They were particularly concerned about the position of the Association of Art Museum Directors (AAMD) in the United States. They did not want Glenbow's Canadian colleague institutions blacklisted for exhibitions or loans from the United States because of their association with Glenbow. Glenbow's executive director subsequently had discussions and correspondence with Jay Gates, chairman of the Ethics Committee of the AAMD. Although the AAMD does not agree with Glenbow's deaccessioning, they have no intention of censuring Canadian institutions, and while the CMA has no formal position on deaccessioning, some council members were supportive of Glenbow's deaccessioning and some were not. Although they know that Glenbow intends to preserve the capital realized from the sale of deaccessioned collections, they felt that we should be precise about the use of the income. The council did not wish to endorse the AAMD position of restricting the use of funds to acquisitions only.

As a result of these consultations, a few colleagues urged us not to go ahead with our Deaccessioning Strategy, while some were most supportive. Some felt that we were charting new territory, with the implication that they may follow our lead, but we felt there was further justification for our deaccessioning following the American Association of Museums decision in June 1993 to adopt important changes to the AAM code of ethics, which ended six years of debate. According to its decision, proceeds from the sale of deaccessioned materials must be used for "acquisitions or the direct care of collections." We obtained a legal opinion which reviewed the Glenbow-Alberta Institute Act, by-laws and other documents relating to the province and Glenbow, as well as policy documents, procedural forms and previous legal opinions. In our lawyer's opinion, deaccessioning was authorized because it was necessary for Glenbow to carry out its business mandate and because we were acting reasonably, in good faith, and in the best interests of the people of Alberta. We consulted an accountant about the Canadian Institute of Chartered Accountants (CICA) proposal to capitalize museum and art gallery collections. He was quite firm that the collection is not a financial asset, and it cannot be depreciated over time as occurs with other assets. Collections are comparable to land in this instance. The balance sheet shows the liquid position of an organization—with assets and liabilities. The collection is not a trading asset, and therefore it should not appear on the balance sheet.

MAKING THE DECISION

During the fall of 1992, the curators did intensive work reviewing all of the international collections, determining criteria either to keep or to deaccession collections. This was a rigorous review. We established a range of criteria for deaccessioning and we applied different combinations of criteria to different collections. These criteria included:

- Representativeness/completeness;
- Relevance to Glenbow's mandate and/or national importance;
- Documentation/provenance;
- Condition;
- Effective use/current and future exhibition, research, interpretation, public use; and
- Ethics especially related to ethnographic collection.

We made a policy decision to deaccession our entire collection of books and art relating to natural history. Glenbow is a human history museum and these natural history collections were an anomaly. This material had been seldom exhibited in the over 30 years it was at Glenbow and there was almost no public or scholarly interest in it. As it was outside of our core mandate, we felt that this collection was appropriate for deaccessioning.

For our African collections in the Ethnology Department we used different criteria. We have an important West African collection of about 5,000 objects, with depth and breadth in various cultural groups, and we had made a commitment to mount a permanent exhibit from this collection as part of a project to feature some of our international collections. There are significant academic links between the University of Calgary and West Africa in the fields of archaeology and anthropology, as well as important links through the oil industry. For this reason, we felt it important to keep and showcase this collection. However, our North, South and East African collections are small and fragmentary, and they are not representative of the scope of material culture in these areas. The collections are not substantial in themselves, nor in relation to each other or West Africa, and do not provide any useful comparative material for study. They lack strong links in our community, and we therefore felt these, too, were suitable collections to deaccession.

The military history collection of 26,000 pieces, spanning nearly five centuries of history, is the largest and most diverse in Western Canada. As the collection is truly international in scope, we decided to deaccession only those objects which do not have provenance and for which there are better quality pieces, as a way of focusing and upgrading this collection. The cultural history collections reflect a broad spectrum of life, work and leisure in Western Canada, from the beginning of the settlement period to the present. The strength of this collection is the story it can tell about settlement in Western Canada, and therefore provenance was the most important factor. Objects which were without provenance, or with provenance unrelated to Western Canada, as well as those which were of low quality or duplicates, were deemed suitable for deaccessioning.

In the process of reviewing the international collections, we established clear reasons to keep certain international collections. Our American illustrator art collection, for example, is one of the most important and largest collections in North America. It is a unique study collection with many fine works and includes some important Canadian artists. Objects are loaned for American exhibitions, and we have mounted four from this collection in the last decade. This is an important collection to keep at Glenbow. However, by November 1992, we had identified 14 collections for potential deaccessioning and had listed objects and prepared estimates of value for nine of these collections. They were:

■ European natural history and sporting subjects—primarily 19th-century British;

■ Natural history illustrated books—primarily 19th-century European;

■ Selected European firearms, edged weapons and ship models;

■ Selected European clocks and watches, decorative arts and penny arcade games;

■ Malvina Hoffman sculpture;

■ Contemporary southwestern rugs and blankets, jewellery and pottery;

■ North, East and South African ethnographic items;

■ Selected ethnographic objects from the upper Amazon; and

■ Contemporary Australian and Pacific Islands ethnographic items.

These nine collections included approximately 3,000 objects, or 0.4 percent of our collections, with an estimated value of $5 million. The deaccessioning and disposal was to proceed over a five-year period.

Throughout the fall of 1992, as we continued our work, we held regular informal meetings with our board of governors on our six guiding operational strategies. These sessions were important to building support and understanding. We also met with staff and volunteers regularly. The six strategies were presented to our board of governors on 17 December 1992. Due to our careful preparation through the fall, we had full board support and approval to proceed.

IMPLEMENTING THE STRATEGY

In January 1993, we began the intensive work for the Deaccessioning Strategy. It is most important to emphasize that at no time did Glenbow's board of governors direct the selections of collections. All decisions were made by the staff. We reviewed preliminary lists prepared in the fall and all donations were removed from the lists. Our source files were combed for information on each and every object to see if there were any legal or statutory restrictions. The board of governors had advised us to keep a small group of representative works from collections which we had planned to deaccession in their entirety, and these representative works were set aside. All of this work was done against a background of great stress, as one of the six strategies was to restructure Glenbow in order to position us to be more effective in the face of what we accepted would be constant change in the 1990s. Consequently, on 23 February 1993, 31 full-time staff lost their jobs and 11 positions went to part-time, and in March 1993 the final lists for the first four collections had been selected by the curators and approved by the director of collections and the executive director. They were presented to the Collections Management Committee of our board and approved for deaccessioning. Their decision was subsequently endorsed by the board.

From the beginning of this work, we had a strong interest in the objects remaining in Canada. In an attempt to keep Glenbow objects in the public domain, we sent letters to 92 institutions in June 1993, offering them the opportunity to purchase items from the nine collections. We also advertised in the Canadian Museums Association's journal *Muse*, in case there were museums or individuals who had not been aware of our deaccessioning. There was a modest response. Thirty-two museums replied, 19 indicating no interest and 13 indicating possible interest. In subsequent follow-up, we have sold some items to Canadian institutions.

In June of 1993, we also held our review of the proposals to sell the natural history art and books, which included nearly 1,000 items. The review panel included the present author, by then director of collections, the executive director, the chairman of the Collections Management Committee (Fred Valentine), the librarian (Lindsay Moir), and Barbara Tyler, director of the McMichael Canadian Collection. The purpose of including someone from outside the museum was to obtain yet another professional perspective on the deaccessioning, as well as advice on any related concerns, including moral and ethical issues. We also wanted their professional opinion in reaching the business decision which was in the best interests of Glenbow. Recognizing the quality of these collections, Sotheby's and Christie's had sent experts from Toronto, New York and London to review them. We received two proposals for the sale of the natural history books and three for the sale of the natural history art, one from an independent dealer in London.

The decision was difficult as there were many factors to weigh. Finally, after lengthy deliberations, we made what we felt was the best business decision and Sotheby's was selected. In the fall of 1993 we submitted applications for cultural property export permits. These permits were granted.

By mid-September of 1993, the press became interested in Glenbow's deaccessioning and we gave more than a dozen print, radio and TV interviews, including *Maclean's* magazine, the *Calgary Herald* and CBC's "Morningside" with Peter Gzowski. The press was very fair in its reporting, although some of the headlines were provocative, and there were very few negative responses as a result of this media coverage. The government of Alberta is our partner, providing just less than half of our funding. During 1993 we had regular discussions with the provincial government, explaining our six strategies, including deaccessioning. In the late summer, Glenbow's deaccessioning had become controversial and members of Cabinet were concerned about the use of the funds realized from deaccessioning. In addition, some people believed that deaccessioned collections should stay in the public domain and be donated to other institutions in Alberta. We subsequently did a presentation to the Standing Policy Committee of the provincial government in Edmonton and, on 13 December 1993, we received formal approval to proceed with our plan.

Sotheby's in New York, 23 April 1994, held a single owner sale of Glenbow's natural history books. The 38 lots were exhibited for a week before the sale and a reception was held for clients. The sale was planned to take advantage of the New York Antiquarian Book Fair when many distinguished collectors and dealers were in town. Thirty-two of the 38 lots were sold in half an hour, realizing $770,965 Canadian.

In June, three ethnographic collections were approved for deaccessioning, including the Southwest collection from the United States, the North, East, and South African collections, and the Australian and Pacific Islands collection. From each of these ethnology collections, we retained a good representative grouping. The Southwest collection to be deaccessioned included 629 items from a total collection of 900 items—rugs, blankets, pottery, and jewellery from the Apache, Navaho and Pueblo cultures. The collection is unexceptional and represents a tourist grade with no ethical implications apart from the Kachinas, which were withdrawn. The deaccessioning of these artifacts will not affect Glenbow's prestige as a holder of significant North American native artifacts. Half of the 400 objects in the collection from North, East, and South Africa have also been deaccessioned. From the Australian and Pacific Islands collection, we have deaccessioned over one-third of the 1,500 items in the collection. This is an eclectic collection of weapons, clothing, ceremonial objects and items for the tourist trade. The portion of the collection we are keeping reflects the variety of artifact types within the collection as a whole, and provides a good core for comparative purposes.

Also, in June 1993, we held meetings to review the proposals to sell the Southwest and Malvina Hoffman sculpture collections. The Southwest collection was sold outright to a Canadian dealer affiliated with an American dealer in Santa Fe, and for the Malvina Hoffman collection we have selected a dealer in New York who will have the collection to sell over a period of 18 months. Subsequently, during late summer 1994, decisions were made about the disposal of the Cultural History and Military History collections. These were sold by auction in Calgary, Red Deer, San Francisco and New York in the winter and spring of 1995. At the first sale of natural history art, 45 objects were sold at the Gleneagles Hotel, Scotland, in late August 1994, while in November there was a large single owner sale of natural history art at Sotheby's in London. To date, we have realized [circa] $2.3 million for the Collections Endowment Fund.

DEACCESSIONING IN REVIEW

We intend to be strict in the use of the income from the endowment funds raised from deaccessioning. The income from the Collections Endowment will be applied only to collections care and documentation, and the endowment will be indexed to protect it from inflation for future purchases for the collections. All of Glenbow's deaccessioning is thoroughly documented, and catalogue records have been changed to reflect the disposal of objects. Over the course of the past two and a half years, we have received positive comments on our Deaccessioning Strategy from professional colleagues and members of the public. We have also had some criticism, including two letters to Glenbow from members of the public, and we have heard of other criticism second-hand. The community is certainly not silent in this matter! However, due to our responsible approach, careful planning and consultation, this criticism has not had a negative impact on Glenbow. Donors have not been adversely affected by the deaccessioning and we continue to receive important gifts of material related to our core mandate.

Deaccessioning of collections is not about lowering standards. It is dependent on good judgment and responsibility, and on being true to core values and beliefs. These are the same attitudes which should guide our acquisitions. In the past, there has been a great deal of mindless collecting along with poor documentation and inadequate care in public collections. Deaccessioning is about making difficult but realistic decisions in the interests of the museum and its community. Stewardship means being entrusted with the management of another's property and preserving that inheritance. It does not mean keeping everything in a collection for all time. As Sir Roy Strong, former director of the Victoria and Albert Museum in London, said, "How can museums function properly if they are going to carry on collecting from here to eternity?"[7] He went on to say, "What we should be doing instead is assessing our collections, refusing some, closing others, and even more important, putting what we have in good order."[8] We no longer have the resources for the proper long-term care and management of collections not germane to our purpose. Through deaccessioning, we believe in ensuring the prudent application of our resources and maintaining public confidence.

Since the 1980s, Glenbow has become more strict and focused in its collecting. We have clearly articulated and detailed collecting plans, policies and procedures to guide our work. In recent years we have reviewed our collections documentation and are upgrading some collections. We have plans to introduce a more efficient in-house computerized collections management system in 1996. We have also begun a long-term storage project to upgrade our cultural history collection, the first phase of which is already complete and has provided new compact storage for our folk studies collection. However, collections are not absolute entities. By continuing to add to them, we change their character and emphasis. As the demographics of communities change, museums must reconsider and refocus their collections. The dramatic recent political changes in South Africa are necessitating a radical rethinking of the content, purpose and meaning of collections. At Glenbow, we believe that we must continue to refine and collect in areas appropriate to our core mandate in order to maintain the vitality of the museum. Deaccessioning and disposal are direct consequences of acquisition. We do not believe it is a viable option to stop collecting and we do not have the option of continually expanding our facilities or staff to accommodate new collections. Museums cannot be static, fixed institutions. They must be dynamic and respond to our changing environment. At Glenbow, we have learned a great deal about our First Nations collections in recent years. As museum professionals, we now handle and care for sacred material in storage in ways that were unheard of even five years ago. We have also placed sacred material on long-term loan in nontraditional environments with First Nations individuals who have the spiritual rights to this material.

Work on the Deaccessioning Strategy will be ongoing, as we finalize the review and sale of approximately 3,000 items from nine collections. The most complex from an ethical point of view must still be considered in depth—the South American collection. Some of this collection is unique and was purchased directly from cultural groups in the Upper Amazon. We must carefully review the implications, and it may be that we will conclude that it is not appropriate to deaccession this collection. Nevertheless, through this Deaccessioning Strategy, we have much more closely defined the scope of our international collections and focused these to provide a better overall direction for all the collections. We have also guaranteed a level of care and maintenance for the collections in the future through establishing the Collections Endowment Fund.

Notes

1. Deaccessioning is the process by which objects are legally removed from the collections through the recommendation of professional staff and approval by the Collections Management Committee and the board of governors. After this, objects are disposed of by various means, including sale.

2. H. Dempsey, 1991. "Treasures of the Glenbow Museum," Glenbow, Calgary, p. 14.

3. E. Tolmatch, 1990. "A Case Study: The Deaccession and Disposal Controversy at the New Brunswick Museum (1985-1990)," *Muse*, 8, 24.

4. E. Tolmatch, 1990. "Selected Bibliography on Deaccessioning," *Muse*, 8, 57.

5. R. Bitner and D. Richeson, 1990. "Artifact Deaccessioning and Disposal of the Saskatchewan Western Development Museum 1984-1988," *Muse*, 8, 35-37.

6. E. Tolmatch, 1990. "A Case Study: The Deaccession and Disposal Controversy at the New Brunswick Museum (1985-1990)," *Muse*, 8, 20-27.

7. Sir Roy Strong, 1985. "What Crisis?" In *Museums*, Art Documents, London, p. 4.

8. Sir Roy Strong, 1985. "The Museum Game." In *Museums*, Art Documents, London, p. 6.

College Art Association (CAA)

RESOLUTION CONCERNING THE SALE AND EXCHANGE OF WORKS OF ART BY MUSEUMS

1. The College Art Association, a national organization which includes in its membership artists, art historians, curators, collectors, dealers and critics, is primarily concerned with scholarship and the teaching of the history and the practice of art. This concern necessarily extends to the acquisition, conservation, display, interpretation and disposal of works of art by museums, as well as to the availability of relevant information about works of art in public collections. Because of this concern, recent developments in the movement of works of art from public to private collections and from collections in the United States to others abroad have made it imperative to develop this resolution.

2. Objects in tax-exempt institutions are held in trust for the public. In this sense they are the cultural property of the public, both present and future. Therefore, every attempt should be made to keep significant works of art, existing in museums, accessible to the public.

3. It is recognized that museum collections occasionally may be strengthened by the wise and constructive sale and exchange of previously acquired works of art and that sale and exchange may be necessitated by the specialized or particular nature of some American museums. Nevertheless, certain principles of sale and exchange are applicable to *all* museums and should be followed if the present educational value of public collections is to be preserved and enlarged.

The "Resolution Concerning the Sale and Exchange of Works of Art by Museums" was adopted by the College Art Association Board of Directors on Nov. 3, 1973. Reproduced with permission.

4. If the work to be removed from a collection would be a desirable acquisition for another public institution, full consideration should be given to making the work directly available for acquisition by such an institution.

5. Procedures for the sale or exchange by museums of a work of art should be far more stringent than those for acquisition. While an acquired work remains in the collection and can be subjected to revised judgment as to its quality and value, a work disposed of can normally be given no second consideration by the museum concerned. Every museum should have clearly formulated policies concerning the sale or exchange of works of art, and such policies should be available to the public. The requirement of at least two-thirds favorable vote by the trustees would be an advisable stipulation of such policies.

6. The board of directors or trustees of a museum carries overall responsibility for its general health. Trustees must, however, invest the professional staff with the primary responsibility for developing the judgments involved in the disposal of a specific work of art. Obviously it is impossible for all museums to have staff experts in all fields. Curators and directors should seek out the best possible advice, consulting recognized experts in the specific field concerned. Even when such specialists are on the museum's staff, it may be advantageous to consult outside experts, both scholars and artists, on the advisability of the action, its impact on the public and the scholarly community and the correctness of the market assessment. While dealers may be involved in the sale or exchange of works of art from a museum collection, they might serve best as agents rather than purchasers.

7. Collections must be considered in terms of their lasting values, and every care should be taken not to allow judgments to be swayed by fluctuations of market values or changing tastes. Moreover, works of art should be considered for sale or exchange only for the purpose of expanding or increasing the importance of the collection, not for operating expenses or building funds.

8. Museums should not accept donations that carry with them conditions they cannot reasonably expect to honor. Removals should be permitted only where no legal obligations imposed by the donor are

in force; where moral obligations are involved they must be evaluated within a moral context. Consultation with near relatives or locatable heirs is always a generous and wise procedure and should include a consideration of the use of the donor's name for the new acquisition.

9. It is important that the disposal of works of art should not inhibit the advancement of scholarly knowledge. When a work of art, after due consideration, has been removed from a museum collection, that museum should retain a full file on the work and continue to make it available to scholars on request. Each file should include photographs, laboratory reports and full information on the disposition of the work. We believe that it is in the interest of dealers to advance scholarly knowledge concerning works of art, and therefore expect them to cooperate in providing information if they are party to disposal transactions. Further, informative statements concerning the sale or exchange of works of art should routinely be included in the periodic public reports of museums. More detailed information should be available on request.

Committee

Joshua C. Taylor, chair

Anne Coffin Hanson

Gilbert S. Edelson

Albert Elsen

Louis Finkelstein

Sherman E. Lee

American Association for State and Local History (AASLH)

Statement of Professional Ethics: Collections

Historical collections, including structures, are the bedrock upon which the practice of history rests. Association members shall always act to preserve the physical and intellectual integrity of their collections.

A. Institutions shall maintain and abide by comprehensive collections policies officially adopted by their governing authorities.

B. Priority shall be given to the care and management of collections.

C. Collections shall not be capitalized or treated as financial assets.

D. Collections shall not be deaccessioned or disposed of in order to provide financial support for institutional operations, facilities maintenance, or any reason other then the preservation or acquisition of collections.

E. Collections shall be acquired, cared for, and interpreted with sensitivity to their cultural origins.

This excerpt concerning collections is taken from the American Association for State and Local History's Statement of Professional Ethics *(1992). Reproduced with permission.*

American Association of Museums (AAM)

Code of Ethics for Museums: Collections

The distinctive character of museum ethics derives from the ownership, care, and use of objects, specimens, and living collections representing the world's natural and cultural common wealth. This stewardship of collections entails the highest public trust and carries with it the presumption of rightful ownership, permanence, care, documentation, accessibility, and responsible disposal.

Thus, the museum ensures that:

- collections in its custody support its mission and public trust responsibilities

- collections in its custody are protected, secure, unencumbered, cared for, and preserved

- collections in its custody are accounted for and documented

- access to the collections and related information is permitted and regulated

- acquisition, disposal, and loan activities are conducted in a manner that respects the protection and preservation of natural and cultural resources and discourages illicit trade in such materials

- acquisition, disposal, and loan activities conform to its mission and public trust responsibilities

- disposal of collections through sale, trade, or research activities is solely for the advancement of the museum's mission. Proceeds from the sale of nonliving collections are to be used con-

This section concerning collections is excerpted from the American Association of Museums's Code of Ethics for Museums *(1994).*

sistent with the established standards of the museum's discipline, but in no event shall they be used for anything other than acquisition or direct care of collections.

■ the unique and special nature of human remains and funerary and sacred objects is recognized as the basis of all decisions concerning such collections

■ collections-related activities promote the public good rather than individual financial gain.

Association of Art Museum Directors (AAMD)

PROFESSIONAL PRACTICES IN ART MUSEUMS

The Collection
Paragraph 24

Disposal of works of art from a museum's collection by sale, exchange, or otherwise, requires particularly rigorous examination and should be pursued with great caution. Although there are circumstances in which disposal of works of art can contribute to the strengthening of a collection, such disposal must be related to the museum's written policy rather than to exigencies of the moment. The procedure for any deaccessioning and sale or exchange should be at least as strict as that for purchasing works of art. The director must provide full justification to the board, with whom the final action rests, and the reasoning should be recorded with particular care. Because development of the collection was the initial intent of the donor of an object or of the funds for acquisition, the moneys (principal and interest) received from the sale of any accessioned work of art must be used only to acquire other works of art. (Similarly, funds received from insurance claims for the loss of a work of art shall be used only for new acquisitions.) (See Appendix B.)

Appendix B

Considerations for Formulating a Policy for Deaccessioning and Disposal
Adopted by the membership of the Association of Art Museum Directors, Jan. 23, 1987; amended 1991.

This selection concerning collections is excerpted from "Professional Practices in Art Museums" (1991) and is reproduced courtesy of the Association of Art Museum Directors.

The governing body of a prudently and responsibly administered art museum should adopt a written policy pertaining to the deaccessioning and disposal of works of art from its collection. This policy should be a clearly integrated part of a comprehensive policy governing institutional purposes and collecting goals.

The deaccessioning and the disposal of a work of art from a museum's collection require exceptional care and should reflect policy rather than reaction to the exigencies of a particular moment. Standards applied to deaccessioning and disposal *must* be at least as stringent as those applied to the acquisition process and should not be subject to changes in fashion and taste.

I.   Purpose of Deaccessioning and Disposal

A. Deaccessioning and disposal may be a legitimate part of the formation and care of collections and, if practiced, should be intended to refine and improve the quality and appropriateness of the collections.

B. Deaccessioning and disposal by sale shall not serve to provide operating funds, and the proceeds from disposal must be treated as acquisition funds.

II.   Criteria for Deaccessioning and Disposal

There are a number of reasons why deaccessioning and disposal might be contemplated. Primary among these are:

A. The object is of poor quality, either intrinsically or relatively, in comparison with other objects of the same type in the collection. Items of modest quality, however, may have sufficient study value to warrant retention.

B. The object is redundant or is a duplicate that has no value as part of a series.

C. The museum's possession of the item is not legitimate, i.e., the work may have been stolen or illegally exported or imported in violation of applicable state and U.S. federal laws. The means of disposal will be determined on a case-by-case basis.

D. The authenticity, attribution, or genuineness of the object is determined to be false or fraudulent, and the object lacks sufficient aesthetic merit or art historical importance to warrant retention. A forgery should be so marked indelibly as such and shall never be returned to the market.

E. The physical condition of the object is so poor that restoration is impossible or will render the object essentially false. Objects damaged beyond reasonable repair that are not of use for study or teaching purposes may be destroyed.

III. Authority and Process

A. Deaccessioning and disposal must comply with all applicable local, state and U.S. federal laws in force at the time, and must observe any terms and obligations which pertained to the acquisition of the work by the museum.

B. The final authority to deaccession and dispose of works of art will rest with the governing body of the institution.

C. The process of deaccessioning and disposal is initiated by the appropriate professional staff with full justification in writing to the director, who will, after appropriate review of the facts and circumstances, present the request to the governing authority.

1. The director shall exercise care to assure that the recommendations are based on authoritative expertise.

2. Third-party review and appraisal are recommended in the case of objects of substantial value.

3. In the case of work(s) by a living artist, special consideration may apply.

D. The director and/or appropriate professional staff shall recommend the time and method of disposal.

E. No member of a museum's board of trustees, governing body, staff, or those whose association with the institution might give them advantage in acquiring the work, shall be permitted to acquire directly or indirectly a work deaccessioned by the museum, or otherwise to benefit from its sale or trade. (Also see Paragraph 25 and Appendix A.)

F. No action pertaining to deaccessioning and disposal should be undertaken which would impair the integrity and good standing of the institution within its community at large and within the profession.

G. Complete and accurate records, including photographs and the circumstances of its disposal, should be maintained on each object removed from the collections.

Paragraph 25

Private collecting of works of art by the director, the staff, and other persons employed by or closely connected with the museum, is an appropriate activity and may enhance expertise. However, no collecting by such persons can be tolerated if, in fact or appearance, it conflicts with the interests of the museum and its collecting programs. Because the possibility of conflict exists, the issue should be openly discussed by all those involved and clear guidelines set forth in writing. The museum always must be given the first opportunity to purchase any work of art. The board should also discuss these issues and consider adopting appropriate guidelines. (See Appendix A and Appendix B, III-E.)

Appendix A

A Code of Ethics for Art Museum Directors as Adopted by the Association of Art Museum Directors

Adopted June 1, 1966, and amended in 1972, 1973, 1974, and 1991.

The position of a museum director is one of trust, involving complex responsibilities. It is the moral obligation of a museum director, in implementing the policies of the governing board, to accept and discharge these to the best of his or her ability for the benefit of the institution and the public. It is assumed that, in all activities, the director will act with integrity and in accordance with the highest moral principles; that he or she will assiduously avoid any and all activities which could in any way compromise the position of the director or the institution. It is further assumed that, in all undertakings within the director's jurisdiction, he or she will be personally responsible for the highest standards of performance. The professional integrity of the director should serve as an example to the staff. The director should communicate the contents of this code of ethics, in substance and detail, to the staff upon assuming the position of director, and to candidates for professional staff positions hired subsequent to that occasion before a candidate's acceptance of employment by the museum.

The members of the Association of Art Museum Directors, maintaining that the position of a museum director is dependent upon professional competence and integrity, and that it requires impartiality and a sense of public responsibility, especially in the area of museum acquisitions, declare that it is unprofessional for museum directors:

A. To use their influence or position in the art world for personal gain. Directors should not traffic in works of art for monetary reasons, nor be party to the recommendation for purchase by museums or collectors of works of art in which the director has any undisclosed financial interest, nor should the director accept any commission or compromising gift from any seller or buyer of works of art. If the director collects art, extraordinary discretion is required to assure that no conflict of interest arises between the director's collecting activity and the concerns of the museum. If such an occasion should arise, it must be resolved by granting the museum's governing board the first option to acquire the work or works of art in question (Also see Paragraph 25 and Appendix B, III-E);

B. To give, for a fee or on a retainer, any certificate or statement as to the authenticity of authorship of a work of art, or any statement of the monetary value of a work of art, except where authorized by and in accordance with the lawful purposes of the museum, or of other nonprofit institutions concerned, or of government agencies;

C. To acquire knowingly or allow to be recommended for acquisition any object that has been stolen, removed in contravention of treaties and international conventions to which the United States is a signatory, or illegally imported into the United States.

D. To dispose of accessioned works of art in order to provide funds for purposes other than acquisitions of works of art for the collection (in accordance with Paragraph 24).

Infractions of these canons of professional conduct, when duly established, will render an art museum director subject to discipline by reprimand, suspension, or expulsion from the association, and/or a director's institution subject to sanctions such as suspension of loans and shared exhibitions.

IV. Selection of Methods of Disposal

The following may be taken into account in selecting a method of disposal:

A. Preferred methods of disposal are sale through publicly advertised auction, sale to or exchange with another public institution, or sale through a reputable, established dealer. Every effort should be taken to identify and evaluate the various advantages and yields available through different means of disposal.

B. In the case of a work of art by a living artist, special consideration might be given to an exchange with the artist.

C. In general, the disposal of an object, whether by sale or exchange, shall be conducted with a view toward maximizing the advantage and yield to the institution, without, however, compromising the highest standards of professional ethics, the institution's standing in its community, or its responsibilities to the donor and the artist.

V. Interest of Donors and Living Artists

A. It is advisable to notify the donor of a work under consideration for deaccessioning and disposal. Circumstances may warrant extending similar courtesy to the heirs of a donor.

B. When a donated object is disposed of, the object newly acquired as a result of the proceeds should acknowledge the original donor(s).

C. When a work of art by a living artist is deaccessioned, consideration must be given to notifying the artist.

Addendum to Appendix B

The AAMD recognizes that part of the mandate of a contemporary arts organization is to expand the definition of what constitutes a work of art as well as question traditional exhibition practices. Therefore, if the organization's written policy provides for the sale of accessioned works, the funds derived from such sales may in exceptional cases be used for purposes analogous to the purchase of works of art, specifically the creation of new works including some which may be non-collectible. Expenditure of these funds for general operating purposes must be precluded.

International Council of Museums (ICOM)

CODE OF PROFESSIONAL ETHICS

DISPOSAL OF COLLECTIONS

4.1. General Presumption of Permanence of Collections

By definition, one of the key functions of almost every kind of museum is to acquire objects and keep them for posterity. Consequently, there must always be a strong presumption against the disposal of specimens to which a museum has assumed formal title. Any form of disposal, whether by donation, exchange, sale or destruction requires the exercise of a high order of curatorial judgment and should be approved by the governing body only after full expert and legal advice has been taken.

Special considerations may apply in the case of certain kinds of specialized institutions such as "living" or "working" museums, and some teaching and other educational museums, together with museums and other institutions displaying living specimens, such as botanical and zoological gardens and aquaria, which may find it necessary to regard at least part of their collections as "fungible" (i.e., replaceable and renewable). However, even here there is a clear ethical obligation to ensure that the activities of the institution are not detrimental to the long-term survival of examples of the material studied, displayed or used.

4.2. Legal or other Powers of Disposal

The laws relating to the protection and permanence of museum collections, and to the power of museums to dispose of items from their

This excerpt pertaining to the disposal of collections is taken from the International Council of Museums' (ICOM) Code of Professional Ethics *(1996) and is reproduced courtesy of ICOM.*

collection, vary greatly from country to country, and often from one museum to another within the same country. In some cases no disposals of any kind are permitted, except in the case of items that have been seriously damaged by natural or accidental deterioration. Elsewhere, there may be no explicit restriction on disposals under general law.

Where the museum has legal powers permitting disposals, or has acquired objects subject to conditions of disposal, the legal or other requirements and procedures must be fully complied with. Even where legal powers of disposal exist, a museum may not be completely free to dispose of items acquired: where financial assistance has been obtained from an outside source (i.e., public or private grants, donations from a friends of the museum organization, or private benefactor), disposal would normally require the consent of all parties who had contributed to the original purchase.

Where the original acquisition was subject to mandatory restrictions these must be observed unless it can be clearly shown that adherence to such restrictions is impossible or substantially detrimental to the institution. Even in these circumstances the museum can only be relieved from such restrictions through appropriate legal procedures.

4.3. Deaccessioning Policies and Procedures
Where a museum has the necessary legal powers to dispose of an object the decision to sell or otherwise dispose of material from the collections should only be taken after due consideration, and such material should be offered first, by exchange, gift or private treaty sale, to other museums before sale by public auction or other means is considered. A decision to dispose of a specimen of work of art, whether by exchange, sale or destruction (in the case of an item too badly damaged or deteriorated to be restorable) should be the responsibility of the governing body of the museum, not of the curator of the collection concerned acting alone. Full records should be kept of all such decisions and the objects involved, and proper arrangements made for the preservation and/or transfer, as appropriate, of the documentation relating to the object concerned, including photographic records where practicable.

Neither members of staff, nor members of the governing bodies, or members of their families or close associates, should ever be permitted to purchase objects that have been deaccessioned from a collection. Similarly, no such person should be permitted to appropriate in any way items from the museum collections, even temporarily, to any personal collection or for any kind of personal use.

4.4. Return and Restitution of Cultural Property

If a museum should come into possession of an object that can be demonstrated to have been exported or otherwise transferred in violation of the principles of the UNESCO Convention on the Means of Prohibiting and Preventing the Illicit Import, Export and Transfer of Ownership of Cultural Property (1970) and the country of origin seeks its return and demonstrates that it is part of the country's cultural heritage, the museum should, if legally free to do so, take responsible steps to cooperate in the return of the object to the country of origin.

In the case of requests for the return of cultural property to the country of origin, museums should be prepared to initiate dialogues with an open-minded attitude on the basis of scientific and professional principles (in preference to action at a governmental or political level). The possibility of developing bilateral or multilateral cooperation schemes to assist museums in countries which are considered to have lost a significant part of their cultural heritage in the development of adequate museums and museum resources should be explored.

Museums should also respect fully the terms of the Convention for the Protection of Cultural Property in the Event of Armed Conflict (The Hague Convention, 1954), and in support of this convention, should in particular abstain from purchasing or otherwise appropriating or acquiring cultural objects from any occupied country, as these will in most cases have been illegally exported or illicitly removed.

4.5. Income from Disposal of Collections

Any moneys received by a governing body from the disposal of specimens or works of art should be applied solely for the purchase of additions to the museum collections.

Milwaukee Public Museum

I. ACCESSION POLICY

A. Requirements for Accession

The museum's accession policy is one of selective acquisition. In the absence of unusual circumstances, as discussed below, no object or specimen shall be accepted or otherwise acquired and added to the museum's permanent collections unless it meets all of the following criteria:

1. It is of such nature and quality as to be consistent with and in furtherance of the accomplishment of the museum's mission as that mission is defined from time to time.

2. To the extent foreseeable at the time of its accession, it can be expected that it will remain permanently in the museum's collection.

3. Its accession will result in an improvement either of a specific existing collection or of the museum's collections viewed as a whole.

4. It will be possible for it to be adequately stored, conserved and cared for.

5. Its desirability as an addition to the museum's collections is sufficient to warrant both the storage space and care.

It is recognized that circumstances can exist where the museum should, at least temporarily, acquire an object that does not meet all of the above criteria. An example is where such an article is a

---

These excerpts are taken from the Milwaukee Public Museum's (MPM) collections policy that was approved by the MPM Collections Committee, board of directors, and Milwaukee County Board in 1994. The sections on deaccessionin, and the teaching collections addendum policy were revised in 1995. All are reprinted with permission from the museum.

part of a desirable larger collection which can only be acquired as a whole. Another example would be an article of significant scientific importance which, although not germane to the museum's collections, must be acquired in order to prevent the loss of its availability to others through private sale, deterioration or destruction. The museum's policy must remain flexible enough for such circumstances to be dealt with on a case-by-case basis. Exceptional acquisitions and those valued over $10,000, however, require the express advance consent of the section head and the president/CEO.

Object/specimen as defined in this document means any tangible item whether natural or man-made or altered. The term "artifact" refers only to objects of or showing human workmanship and does not include specimens of naturally occurring objects.

B. Who Can Approve Accessions

1. Human History Sections

In normal circumstances and subject to the following conditions, the curator in charge of the applicable collection will recommend accessions for approval to the curator's section head. All such accessions must, however, be listed and described in an annual report submitted to the president/CEO and the board of directors, and the president/CEO shall have a continuing responsibility to remain informed concerning all accessions and to determine that they continue to conform to the policies here stated.

2. Natural History Sections

In normal circumstances, an accession requires the approval of the curator in charge of the collection of which the accessioned article will form a part, who will then inform the curator's section head. All such accessions must, however, be listed and described in an annual report submitted to the president/CEO and the directors, and the president/CEO and section head shall have a continuing responsibility to remain informed concerning all accessions and to determine that they continue to confirm to the policies here stated.

Whenever there is reason to believe that an accession could significantly affect the general interests of the museum, as where the article has substantial monetary or publicity value, cultural sensitivity, or where it would require substantial or special storage space, or where its care or conservation would require unusual time or expense, the curator in charge must obtain the advance consent of the section head and the president/CEO before approving its accession. It shall further be the obligation of the president/CEO to determine whether it is desirable or practical for the advance consent of the board of directors also to be obtained. In making such determinations, the curator, the section head, and the president/CEO should resolve any doubts in favor of obtaining a higher-level consent.

C. **Determination of Title**

No object or specimen should be accessioned until the museum has obtained satisfactory assurance that the donor or seller can transfer clear title. Information should be obtained concerning its past history of ownership and how it came into the possession of the donor or seller, and a record of that information should be included in the accession file.

Special diligence should be used to assure that any object was not illegally imported into the United States and that there are no legal, ethical or environmental considerations which would make its accession undesirable.

In all instances, the gift or sale of an object or collection to the museum should be accompanied by a written statement signed by the donor or seller which describes the thing or things being given or sold and which makes it clear that title is being transferred to the museum.

In the case of donated material, this should be in a form approved by the section head, the president/CEO and the registrar; such standard form is a deed of gift. All such documentation should be included in the accession file.

D. **Restrictions or Conditions Imposed by Donor**

It is the general policy of the museum that no object may be accepted unless its ownership by the museum will be free of all restrictions and conditions.

It is recognized that exceptional circumstances can arise where strict enforcement of this general policy would not be in the best interests of the museum. Any such exception must, however, have the advance approval of the curator in charge, the section head, the president/CEO and (if the president/CEO deems it desirable) of the board of directors. In any event, every attempt should be made to hold restrictions or conditions to a practical minimum and to obtain the consent of the donor that the restrictions will terminate after a finite time limit.

If any restrictions or conditions are accepted, they must be in writing executed by both the donor and the museum and must be included in the accession file.

E. Accession Procedures

An accession shall comprise all material formally entered into the permanent collections at the same time. Cultural material accessions are usually from a single source (donor, collector, etc.) acquired by the museum at the same time. Natural history accessions, in some circumstances, may represent multiple source materials processed together as one lot. Accessioning and sectional registration procedures should be completed expeditiously.

All accessions shall be entered in a permanent accessions register by the registrar and be given an accession number. An accession file shall be opened for each accession and shall include all basic documents relevant to the accession. Any additional information will be available in the appropriate museum sections as part of the catalogue procedures.

In all other respects, accessions shall comply with such procedures as shall be developed by the registrar with the approval of the president/CEO and the board of directors.

F. Appraisals

No appraisals of any objects (whether or not donated to the museum) shall be made at any time by any museum personnel, including any member of the board of directors.

Formal appraisals, if any, shall in all instances be obtained by the donor at the donor's expense. The museum may, however, undertake an appraisal on its own behalf of objects already accessioned or as part of the accession process.

G. **Acceptance of Gifts to be Sold by the Museum**

Occasionally a donor may offer to give an object of value to the museum with the contemplation that it will be sold by the museum and the proceeds used for museum purposes.

Such gifts may be accepted, subject to the prior approval of the president/CEO and (if he deems it desirable) by the board of directors.

In such event, the object shall not be accessioned by the museum but shall be temporarily held until the object can be sold in such manner as shall be in the best interests of the museum.

In the case of such gifts, it remains equally important that the museum obtain satisfactory assurance of the donor's title and that transfer of title be in writing signed by the donor. Special diligence should be used to assure that the object was not illegally imported into the United States and that there are no legal, ethical, or environmental considerations which would make its acquisition undesirable.

H. **Acceptance of Specimens to be Shared**

From time to time, the museum will collect specimens jointly with another museum or institution with which it agrees to share the resulting collection.

No such specimen shall be accessioned until a final written agreement has been reached as to which items are to stay with the Milwaukee Public Museum and which are to become the property of the other institution.

When such an agreement has been reached, it should be honored by delivering the agreed specimens to the other institution and by accessioning the remainder.

I. **Teaching Collections**

The museum also collects materials for teaching purposes. The primary teaching collection is maintained by the museum's

Educational Programming Section although many of the curatorial sections also maintain teaching collections. Although these collections may contain accessioned materials, they are generally composed of non-accessioned materials and it is not general policy to add accessioned materials to these collections. Curatorial staff are encouraged to share specimens with and collect for these collections and to direct materials offered for donation which do not meet the "Requirements for Accession" to the Educational Programming Section for possible inclusion in the Teaching Collection. Addendum I: Teaching Collections Policy deals specifically with the Educational Programming Section collection.

II. DEACCESSION POLICY

A. Introduction

The museum's deaccession policy, as formulated and administered from time to time, must seek to strike a practical balance among the following three considerations:

1. The fiduciary obligations with respect to the preservation of its collections which Milwaukee County, the board of directors, and the museum staff owe to persons who have donated to those collections as a public trust and for those individuals for whose benefit the museum has undertaken to preserve the museum's collection.

2. The museum's need periodically to renew and alter its collection policies.

3. Its need selectively to refine its existing collections in order that they may remain consistent with these policies.

To this end, the museum has a continuing obligation to review and evaluate the strengths and weaknesses of its existing collections, and in light of such evaluation, to reformulate and restate in writing its overall collections policy.

B. Conditions Warranting Deaccession

No article, consisting of an artifact or specimen included in the museum's collections, shall be deaccessioned unless it meets at least one of the following criteria:

1. Its retention would be inconsistent with the character of the museum's collections as a whole and with its current policies and objectives with respect to those collections.

2. In the opinion of staff, it either lacks authenticity or is so lacking in documentation as to render it valueless for purposes of scholars or public education.

3. It is a duplicate or of inferior quality to another identical or similar article in the museum's collections.

4. It cannot be adequately stored or cared for.

5. It is in such bad condition or in such a bad state of deterioration that it is useless as a part of the museum's collections.

6. The possibility exists for it to be traded for some other (and usually similar) article which would be substantially more needed in and more consistent with the museum's collections.

7. Articles may be deaccessioned and repatriated when and where appropriate in keeping with the Native American Graves Protection and Repatriation Act and any other relevant governmental laws or acts.

C. Who Can Authorize Deaccession

1. Approvals

The article intended for deaccession shall be given an estimated dollar value by the curator in charge of the collection, and the president/CEO must concur in this valuation.

If the valuation is less than $1,000, deaccession may be authorized by the president/CEO. If the valuation is $1,000 or more, deaccession must also have the approval of the museum's board of directors and the Milwaukee County Board of Supervisors.

2. Native American Collections

If the proposed deaccession is of Native American origin, deaccession must also have the approval of the museum's board of directors and the Milwaukee County Board of Supervisors, regardless of value.

3. Natural History Collections

Curators in the natural sciences may be authorized by the vice president of collections and research to negotiate minor deaccessions of damaged material, those which have lost their provenience, or small quantities of specimens being retained by scholars at other institutions as part of the routine arrangement for many research loans.

D. Obligation to Donor

If an article intended for deaccession was obtained by the museum subject to restrictions which are inconsistent with deaccession, and if the donor is still living, every attempt shall be made to obtain from the donor a written waiver of such restrictions and a consent to its deaccession. If the donor refuses to provide such a waiver, the museum must abide by the terms of the original accession agreement. If the donor is no longer living, it will be necessary to consult legal counsel as to whether the heirs or the estate of the donor can provide such a waiver in his or her place.

If an article is held by the museum without restriction but its donor is still living, the donor should be informed of the intended deaccession even though it is unnecessary to obtain the donor's consent thereto.

In general, all donors of deaccessioned articles (or their surviving families) should be courteously and tactfully dealt with and kept informed of any such deaccession to the extent deemed necessary and appropriate in the judgment of the president/CEO.

E. Evaluation of Museum's Title

No article may be deaccessioned until it has been established that the museum has clear title to it and has full power and authority to transfer such title to others. Special care should be taken to make certain that it is not held by the museum on loan from some other institution or person.

F. Procedure for Deaccessioning

1. Procedures

Prior to deaccession, an authorization in writing, in a form prepared by the registrar, shall be executed by the curator in charge, the section head, and the president/CEO and placed in the file relating to the original accession of the article involved. In cases where approval of the board of directors is required, a notation of the board's approval shall be entered in its minutes.

In instances where deaccessioning has been delegated to specific curators, notification of deaccessioning in form prepared by the registrar shall be executed by the curator in charge and provided to the section head, the president/CEO, and the registrar.

2. Notification

The president/CEO shall provide the board of directors with annual reports listing all deaccessions made by the museum. The museum corporation shall deliver to the county within 120 days following the end of the year a list of all artifacts deaccessioned in the previous year.

A written memorandum of the facts relating to the disposal of the deaccessioned article, and anything received in exchange or payment therefor, shall be prepared and retained as a permanent record of the museum.

3. Valuations

Those items which in the best estimation of the individual responsible for the material have a value over $500 will be appraised by an outside appraiser qualified to determine the value of similar materials.

Where the deaccession involves a number of related articles, they shall be valued as a group.

G. **Disposition of Deaccessioned Articles**

Articles of minimal value, whenever practical, should after deaccession be available to the museum's Educational Programming Section for use as educational aids. Due to the nature of their use in such programming, they must be considered expendable and such use may result in their ultimate destruction. (See Addendum 1: Teaching Collections Policy.)

1. Gifts

It is customary in some disciplines for scientists who borrow

and identify biological or paleontological specimens to retain
some duplicate examples for the collections of their institution.
Such gifts or specimens usually involve negligible monetary
value. All such transactions shall be in keeping with the norms
of the scientific discipline involved.

2. Exchanges

The formal reciprocal transfer of material or specimens between
two or more institutions, or between an institution and an individual, is desirable if it serves to advance the research, educational, or exhibition programs of both parties. An open exchange
is an ongoing agreement between the Milwaukee Public Museum and another institution. By prior arrangement, the two
institutions agree to exchange material over a long period of
time without concern for simultaneous shipments. Generally,
exchanges are not made unless the material has been studied,
determined, documented, or represents duplicate or out-of-
scope material.

3. Sales

If the section head, in collaboration with the curatorial and collections management staff decides that certain specimens or
collections are no longer needed for the research and exhibition programs of the Milwaukee Public Museum, either current or anticipated, these specimens may be deaccessioned and
sold, subject to the following guidelines.

a. Goals of sales

To bring the best possible price for the material being sold
consistent with our responsibilities for preservation of collections of scientific value.

b. Methods of sales

The preferred type of sale, whenever an appropriate price can
be so obtained, is to another museum or similar nonprofit
institution where the article will continue to be held for the
benefit of the public. If this is not possible, then the sale should,
whenever practical, be by public auction. ONLY in rare
instances, and where necessary in order to obtain an adequate price, should such a sale be made through a private

dealer, and in such instances it should, after formal approval by the board of directors, be made on consignment for sale pursuant to a pre-negotiated commission.

Public auction, sealed bidding, open bidding over a period of time, and consignment with Milwaukee Public Museum shops or other sales outlets, are acceptable options, provided that the availability of such material for sale has been given publicity aimed at the appropriate audience of potential purchasers.

c. Application of proceeds
All funds generated by sales of deaccessioned collections, net of selling costs, shall be placed in the specimen acquisition fund of the section from which the material was withdrawn.

4. Specimen Discard
Removal or culling of undocumented, surplus, or deteriorated specimens, essentially of no scientific or monetary value, from the collections is an acceptable practice. If such specimens are not needed by other museum sections, or cannot be transferred under G.3 above, then they may be destroyed and discarded, in accordance with the museum's "Registration Procedures."

H. Acquisition of Deaccessioned Articles by Museum Personnel
No deaccessioned article may be acquired from the museum by any member of the museum staff or board of directors or by any member of their immediate families. For purposes of this section, the term "immediate families" shall mean the spouse, linear descendant, linear ascendant, brother, or sister of the board member or staff member.

I. Use of Proceeds of Deaccession
Proceeds from the sale of a deaccessioned article shall be used solely for the acquisition of objects for the museum's collections and shall in no event be used to defray its operating expenses, and all such proceeds shall be held in a trust account until they can be so used.

In general, the only permitted use shall be the purchase of a desired addition or additions to the museum's collections, giving priority first to the collections from which the article was deaccessioned, second to other collections in the same department, and third to collections in other departments of the museum.

In special situations, when it is in the best interests of the museum, such proceeds may be used to defray the cost of restoration or conservation of the specific collection or collections, with the priorities being the same as those stated in the preceding paragraph.

It shall be the responsibility of the museum and the registrar to comply with all requirements of applicable federal and state law, including any requirements of the Internal Revenue Service.

ADDENDUM I: TEACHING COLLECTIONS POLICY

The main mission of the Educational Programming Section is to offer a broad array of educational programs and information services to enhance understanding of the collections and exhibits.

A Teaching Collection is maintained to further this mission in keeping with current educational philosophy of discovery learning in museums. A Teaching Collection is a collection of objects that are handled by museum educators, docents, and visitors in museum programs. A Teaching Collection which provides objects to be used in public programming is essential to a successful learning experience. The use of objects which people can manipulate illustrates learning goals in an exciting personally involved method of discovery.

Objects in the Teaching Collection are different from the permanently accessioned objects in the museum. Objects in the Teaching Collection have their own object numbering system, storage strategy, storage conditions and system of use which differ from the permanently accessioned objects.

This document establishes policy for the accessioning of objects to the Teaching Collection of the Milwaukee Public Museum, delineates circumstances and methods by which materials shall be accessioned, loaned or deaccessioned. It shall be the responsibity of the museum to comply with all requirements of applicable federal and state laws.

A. Collections Committee

All matters pertaining to the Teaching Collection are referred to the Educational Programming Section staff. The chairman of the committee is the supervisor of the Educational Programming Section. Issues related to the Teaching Collection are placed the agenda of the weekly sectional meeting. The charge of the committee is to promote the care and utilization of the collection and to plan for growth, replacement or removal.

B. Types of Objects in the Collection

The Teaching Collection will be comprised of objects related to human and natural history which can be used in public programming. Also included are materials which are used in craft activities with children. Objects which are of a sensitive nature, are significant, unique or potentially hazardous to visitors in hands-on programming are not part of the Teaching Collection. Generally, only the most commonly available and duplicate historic objects will be used in demonstration programs. The Educational Programming Section endorses use in its programs of high-quality replicas based on documented originals. Use of original materials will be permitted only if effects of use are carefully and regularly monitored and a museum educator or curator handle the object. Acquisition of objects for the Teaching Collection will be determined on a needs basis.

C. Instructions Concerning Donations to the Museum

1. Items brought in for donation to the museum

a. A receipt and removal form is used to record donor's name, address and phone number; if brought in by a person other than the donor, their name, address and phone number is recorded; the date of receipt is recorded.

b. The receipt and removal form and objects are then given to the appropriate curatorial section for consideration.

c. The donor is told that they are receiving a temporary receipt only and that the donation will not be formally accepted until acted upon by the curatorial section; the donation or part of the donation may be returned or given to the Educational Proramming Section for consideration. The donor is also informed about the purpose and use of a Teaching Collection and is informed that a permanent record will be kept of the deed of gift form.

d. Thanks and appreciation are expressed to the donor for his/her interest in the museum who should be told that one of the collections staff will be in touch soon. The donor should be contacted as soon as a decision is made on the proposed donation.

2. Items brought in specifically for the teaching collection

a. Occasionally, visitors will donate objects with specific wishes that the materials be used for the Teaching Collection. These objects are accepted using a receipt and removal form as above; the donor is informed that a curator will be invited to look at their donation and the education staff will also examine the collection. The donation or part of the donation may be returned, expressions of thanks and appreciation are given and the donor is told that one of the museum staff will be in touch soon.

b. The Educational Programming Section contacts the appropriate curator to look at the donation. If it is rare, significant, unique or needed for the permanently accessioned collections, the donor is informed of the museum's wish to place the objects in the permanent collection. If the object is not appropriate for the permanent collection but is appropriate for the Teaching Collection, the object is placed in the Teaching Collection. If the object is not appropriate for the Teaching Collection, it is returned to the donor.

3. Objects purchased

Objects needed for programs are purchased by the Educational Programming Section staff. Bills of sale are kept and included in the records. Processing of any incoming material will be in accordance with the current Milwaukee Public Museum Pest Management Program.

4. Objects transferred

The Educational Programming Section encourages the transfer of objects from curatorial collections that are deaccessioned due to lack of provenance, lack of fit with collections policy, or other reason stated in their collection policy. Disposals from permanently accessioned collections will be noted and documented.

5. Objects from the permanent collections

Occasionally, objects are found in the Teaching Collection with accession numbers from the permanent collection. In the past, it was a practice to use objects from the permanently accessioned collection in public programming. It is now the practice to return objects to the permanent collections area or to encase them in order to allow safe handling. An internal loan record will be kept of material from other sections in the custody of Educational Programming.

D. Incoming Loans

The Educational Programming Section will accept loans from schools, institutions or individuals offering touchable objects to supplement museum programming or objects to be placed in the Wizard Wing collector's corner showcase. Incoming loans will only be short-term and will only be used by Educational Programming Section staff. All loans will be recorded using the standard Milwaukee Public Museum (MPM) registration procedures (i.e., loan forms will be executed, collection covered by insurance).

On July 1, 1990, the Milwaukee Public Museum Audiovisual Center was closed. Assets were transferred to Media Makers

Inc., later renamed Innovative Media Services. The Milwaukee Public Museum owns title to and has sole possession of the circulating specimen collection. Innovative Media Services distributes the specimen collection. Innovative Media Services allows the Milwaukee Public Museum free, unlimited use of the entire media collection. Objects may be recalled to the museum with no formal loan agreements, since the museum is the sole owner of the circulating specimen collection.

E. Outgoing Loans

Outgoing loans of objects in the Teaching Collection are occasionally arranged for schools, teacher in-service programs, or ethnic festivals in the Milwaukee area. Outgoing loans are arranged and picked up only by written request. If objects will be in danger (exposed to elements, not properly supervised), needed for programming at the Milwaukee Public Museum or used for extended periods of time, outgoing loans may be refused by the Educational Programming Section staff. Only objects from the Teaching Collection which have been catalogued may be considered for loan. Objects must bear a permanent identification number. Loans will be for a specified time period not to exceed three months with review and renewal. Loans from the Teaching Collection may be made to governmental agencies including county government. Loan-out forms established by the registrar for use among other museum loans will be used, following the same procedure, by the Educational Programming Section.

F. Appraisals

The Educational Programming Section staff is expected to be reasonably informed about the fair market value of items in its collection for insurance or replacement purposes. Because of the collector's corner in the Wizard Wing, visitors bring in objects of their own for identification and additional information. The staff does not offer appraisal services to the public, written or verbal. Referrals for appraisals may be given to the public but only if more than one source is suggested, without appearance of favor.

G. Record Keeping

To assist the Educational Programming Section in knowledge of the incoming object, the following information is gathered from the curator or the donor:

1. Deed of gift

    a. What is the name of the object?

    b. Who manufactured it?

    c. Who used the object?

    d. When was the object made? When was it used?

    e. How was the object used?

    f. Where has the object been?

    g. Who owned the object?

    h. If the object was purchased by the Educational Programming Section staff, a bill of sale should be present.

A deed of gift form is completed for the object. One copy is given to the donor. A second copy is kept in the files of the Educational Programming Section. The original is placed in the registrar's deed of gift files.

2. Acknowledgment of gift

The head of the Educational Programming Section will write a personal letter to each donor acknowledging each gift on behalf of the Milwaukee Public Museum. In the case of outstanding or valuable gifts, the registrar and museum president/CEO shall be notified so that appropriate action may be taken over and above the acknowledgement of the Educational Programming Section.

3. Record file

A record file has been created to file all correspondence and documents related to the objects in the Teaching Collection. The file will be placed in the Educational Programming Section office.

4. Object number

A record number for the Teaching Collection shall be different from the permanent collection system. The existing numbering system for the Teaching Collection shall be used. It consists of a series of numbers related to the date of accession. For example, the 32nd anthropological object accessioned in August 1990 would be accessioned as follows: A 8-90-32. India ink will be used for permanent marking of metal, wood and ceramic objects. Textiles will have an accession number sewn on using a number placed on bias tape.

5. Catalogue

There are two types of catalogues, an object card and a donor card. The object card has an individual item, description and donor name. These are filed numerically by object number for each category. The donor card is filed alphabetically. With the accessibility of computers, the catalogue file will be placed on computer.

H. Disposition

Items are removed from the Teaching Collection if they have seriously deteriorated or have been damaged beyond repair through overuse or through time. Items are also removed if they are potentially hazardous to the museum staff and visitors. Items that may be potentially more useful in another museum teaching collection, museum, nonprofit cultural organization or for educational purposes may also be removed from the MPM Teaching Collection and may be transferred to these other institutions.

Objects which are disposed of because of overuse or damage beyond repair will be recorded as "disposed" on the accession card. The reason for disposition will also be recorded on the card.

In some cases, the objects of no further use in educational programming may be exchanged or sold to obtain objects or reproductions or to repair existing materials which are needed in programming. In the case of transferring or exchanging objects, the Educational Programming Section head is notified, the curator of the appropriate related permanent collection is notified, the registrar is contacted, and the president/CEO has the final approval of transfer. A document of transfer is kept in the registrar's office and the office of the Educational Programming Section.

I. Conservation

Preventive conservation will be practiced, i.e., doing everything possible for an object to prevent ongoing deterioration and destruction by problems of material, people or environment. The Educational Programming Section will take the best possible care for the collection to prevent damage to the objects. Since the objects are not meant to be in a permanent collection, the high standards applied to the permanent collection will not be applied to the Teaching Collection.

Objects with record numbers from the Teaching Collection will be repaired by staff and/or volunteers from the Educational Programming Section. Objects from the permanent accession collection used with permission from the curatorial section will be repaired by conservation staff.

J. Replicas

When possible, replicas for use in demonstrations will be based on the original objects in the collections of the Milwaukee Public Museum. Reproductions will be clearly and permanently marked to indicate date and manufacture of reproductions. In using reproductions, the Educational Programming Section will attempt to clearly separate in the public's mind the use of replicas from the exhibition of originals.

K. Code of Ethics

Employment by a museum is a public trust involving great responsibility. In all activities, the Educational Programming Section staff will act with integrity and in accordance with ethical principles as well as the highest standards of objectivity. No employee may use his/her affiliation to promote private collection activities. No employee may participate in dealing for profit in objects related to those in the Teaching Collection.

L. Use of Volunteers in Collections Area

Volunteers will be allowed to use the collections under the supervision of museum educator staff. Volunteers will also be encouraged to assist in accessioning and repairing objects in the Teaching Collection.

M. Inventories

Inventories account for objects in our custody. Inventories facilitate in the administration of the collections, insurance, security and needs list. Inventories will be updated regularly as time and staffing permits.

Cincinnati Museum of Natural History

COLLECTIONS POLICY

SECTION III: DEACCESSIONING

A. Introduction

1) *Deaccessioning* is the formal process used to legally and permanently remove an object from the collections. *Disposition* is the manner in which the museum transfers the object to a new owner or destroys it.

2) When undertaking the deaccession and disposition of specimens, the museum proceeds with the knowledge that it holds its collections as a public trust. In order to fulfill this trust most effectively, the museum must balance considerations of continued public or scientific access to a specimen with the obligation of maximizing the benefit of any transaction to the museum's own collections.

3) The museum has possession of many specimens whose status as collections objects is unclear. For much of its history the museum did not "accession" objects in the modern sense of the word. ("Accessioning" is the act of formally adding an object or objects to a museum's permanent collections. This is distinct from obtaining title to the object, which precedes accessioning, and cataloguing, which traditionally follows it.) For some objects there is insufficient documentation to determine what their original status might have been. For the sake of adhering to the highest possible standards of stew-

In January 1995 the Cincinnati Museum of Natural History merged with the Cincinnati Historical Society and Museum Center Foundation, forming Cincinnati Museum Center. CMC is currently updating this policy, which dates from 1992, to reflect these changes.

ardship, the museum will apply the procedures for disposition of collections outlined in the deaccessioning policy to all such objects of uncertain status.

B. Criteria

The museum may consider deaccessioning objects from the collection that meet any of the following conditions:

1) The object is not relevant to the purpose and scope of the collections as defined in Section I of the Collections Policy.

2) The museum is not able to provide adequate care for the object.

3) The object has deteriorated past the point of usefulness.

4) The type of object is sufficiently represented in the collections, or has been replaced with superior examples.

5) The object is inferior or has substandard documentation.

6) The object is to be traded for an object of equal or greater value for the purpose of improving the collection.

7) The object is an important duplicate (for example, one of a type series) that is being deposited with another institution for the purpose of increasing its accessibility and for risk management.

C. Authority and Responsibility

1) The curator responsible for the department into which the object is catalogued may propose the object for deaccessioning. In the case of objects that were never catalogued into a department, or material from an uncurated department, any curator, the director of collections, or the deputy director for collections and research may make such a proposal.

2) The curator, director of collections, or deputy director for collections and research proposing deaccessioning is responsible for forwarding a written deaccessioning proposal, includ-

ing copies of all known documentation on the object and the proposed method of disposition to the director of collections.

3) The director of collections is responsible for checking the records to locate any known restrictions on the donation, and for investigating any other legal issues affecting deaccession or disposition.

4) A list of proposed deaccessions must be circulated to the deputy directors of all divisions inside the museum. This will determine whether they or their staffs have comments on potential use of the object within the museum that might affect the deaccession or disposal decision.

5) The deaccession proposal must be discussed by the senior staff of the collections and research division, approved by the deputy director for collections and research, and forwarded to the president for approval.

6) The board of trustees shall be notified in a timely manner of deaccessions that have been approved.

7) In the case of deaccessions of particularly valuable, important, or politically sensitive material, the president should bring the deaccession proposal before the board for approval.

8) Material that is de facto deaccessioned by virtue of unintentional destruction may be deaccessioned without following the procedures outlined above. For this material, it is sufficient to inform the director of collections and the deputy director for collections and research in writing of the change in status of the object, and the method of disposition.

D. Notes on Methods of Disposition

1) Acceptable methods of disposition for objects are:

a) Sale at public auction or in the public marketplace.

b) Donation to or exchange with another educational or research nonprofit institution.

c) Transfer to another division within the museum for use in exhibits or education.

d) Destruction.

2) Objects with significant value for research should be offered in sale, exchange, or as a donation to other educational or research nonprofits, with preference to those in this geographical region or to those in a geographical region for which the object has special significance.

3) All methods of disposition must be in compliance with all relevant local, state, federal, and international laws.

4) All specimens must be accompanied with a full disclosure of any known hazard they may present to a future owner.

5) No museum employee, member of the board of trustees, officer, volunteer or business associate shall receive an advantage not available to the general public in the acquisition of an deaccessioned object.

6) If material in a subject area for which there is no expertise on staff is going to be deaccessioned, an appropriate outside consultant must be contacted for advice on methods of disposition, the advisability of obtaining an appraisal, and similar issues.

E. Sales

1) If it is the opinion of the curatorial staff that an object should remain in the public domain, then objects may be offered in sale to appropriate and reputable nonprofit institutions, with this sale being suitably publicized so that the museum obtains the best selling price given the pool of appropriate buyers.

2) Whenever possible, objects that are sold should be offered at public auction at a reserve price. If the reserve price is not met, then the object may be sold privately for at least the reserve price.

3) If the value of the object is too insignificant to warrant its being sold at auction, then the object may be offered for public sale by the museum. This dollar value will be specified in the collections and research division procedures manual, and approved by the deputy director for collections and research.

4) The proceeds from the sale of deaccessioned collections objects will revert to the department in which they were catalogued and may be used only for the acquisition of specimens. "Specimen acquisition" includes purchase, the cost of preparing specimens, or the funding of expeditions for the purpose of collecting specimens. In the case of an object that was not catalogued into the collections, the money shall revert into the department controlling that subject area. In the case of objects that do not fall within any department's subject area, the money shall revert to a collections and research division discretionary fund for the acquisition of specimens.

F. Exchanges

1) Exchanges can be made with reputable nonprofits or for-profit institutions.

2) The museum does not exchange material with private individuals.

3) Exchanges should be for objects of equivalent monetary or intrinsic value. In the case of objects of significant monetary worth, this must be documented by formal appraisals.

G. Donations

1) Collections objects will be donated only to nonprofit educational or research institutions, never to individuals.

H. Destruction

1) If an object has deteriorated to the point that it is of no further use to anyone, or if it constitutes an uncontainable hazard, then it may be destroyed.

2) This destruction must comply with any relevant local, state, or federal regulations concerning disposal of such material and must be conducted in such a way as to pose no public hazard, in the best judgment of the museum.

3) The destruction must be witnessed and attested to in writing by a curator or the director of collections.

I. Records Keeping

1) A complete and permanent record of each deaccession, including documentation of the deaccession and disposition process, will be kept by the director of collections.

2) The museum's identifying numbers will be removed from deaccessioned objects before disposition except in cases (such as transfer to a research institution) where it is necessary and appropriate for the numbers to remain as part of the object's history.

PROCEDURES FOR DEACCESSIONING AND DISPOSAL OF WORKS OF ART

INTRODUCTION

At a special meeting of the board of trustees held on June 20, 1973, the procedures for disposal of works of art from the museum's collections were modified. Since there has been considerable public interest expressed in these procedures, the museum has decided to issue this booklet, which includes the latest modifications.

I. DEACCESSIONING

An explanation of the term "deaccession" as used by the museum seems advisable at the outset. It does not mean sale. It does mean that the appropriate persons at the museum, that is, the trustees or the members of the Acquisitions Committee, have concluded with the aid of staff reports and recommendations and, on occasion, the advice of outside consultants, that an object may be removed from the collection and be further considered for disposal by sale or exchange.

Sometimes, for a variety of reasons, i.e., objection by the donor or his heirs, change of market conditions, or change of professional judgment by the staff, an object previously deaccessioned will be reaccessioned and cannot again be approved for deaccessioning without compliance with the procedures outlined below.

The Metropolitan Museum of Art's procedures for deaccessioning and disposal of works of art date from June 20, 1973. They are reprinted with the permission of the museum.

STEPS FOR DEACCESSIONING

1. The curator of a department recommends deaccessioning of a work of art in his department to the curator-in-chief and the director. If they decide the matter should be considered further the following steps are taken.

2. The museum ascertains, generally with the advice of counsel, that there is no legal restriction against disposal.

(a) The museum will, as in the past, consistently honor legal restrictions attaching to the gift or bequest of any work of art. In addition, requests which do not impose any legal obligation accompanying the bequest or gift of any work of art will be respected to the extent feasible, unless modified by the donor or, if the donor is not living, the donor's heirs or legal representatives, on notice to the attorney general of the state of New York.

(b) No work of art valued by the museum at $10,000 or more will be disposed of within 25 years following its receipt if objected to, after appropriate notice, by the donor or the donor's heirs or legal representatives. This policy will apply to any work of art, including gifts or bequests which are not subject to any legal obligation or accompanied by any non-binding request.

3. Normally, the recommendation is then presented and discussed at a meeting of the curators of all departments, with the curator-in-chief and the director in attendance.

4. After taking account of this discussion, the curator-in-chief and the director make the decision whether or not the work of art should be placed upon the agenda for deaccessions of the Acquisitions Committee of the board.

5. The curator makes a presentation to the Acquisitions Committee. The presentation includes the curator's evaluation of the work. While customarily outside appraisals have been sought when deaccession of works of significant value was under consideration, on June 8, 1972, instructions were given to the staff that if an object proposed for deaccessioning was estimated by

the curator to be worth more than $2,000, two outside appraisals should be presented.

6. The Acquisitions Committee listens to the recommendation of the curator, the curator-in-chief and the director.

7. The committee then decides whether or not to deaccession the object.

8. If the work of art has been evaluated by the museum at $25,000 or less, based upon the best available comparable figures at the time, the vote on deaccessioning by the Acquisitions Committee is final.

9. If the object has been evaluated by the museum at over $25,000, then the vote of the Acquisitions Committee is a recommendation only and must be voted upon either by the executive committee of the board of trustees or the full board, whichever meets next.

After the object has been deaccessioned, there is time for the president, the director, the curator-in-chief, and the curator to re-evaluate the decision, taking once again into consideration all factors leading to the decision to place the object in the deaccession status.

II. DISPOSAL

Steps for Disposal

If it is decided to proceed, then a separate process of disposal, with its appropriate checks and balances, is initiated.

The steps are as follows:

Objects Valued $25,000 or Less

1. Promptly after action by the board of trustees, the Executive Committee or the Acquisitions Committee to deaccession any work of art with a museum valuation in excess of $5,000, notice will be given to the attorney general of the state of New York at least 15 days (unless otherwise agreed upon with the attorney general at the time) prior to the sale or exchange of such work of art, specifying the restrictions, if any, applicable to such work of art.

2. Once an item is deaccessioned by the Acquisitions Committee (value of $25,000 or less), the director, or, at his request, the curator-in-chief, or the curator in charge of the department which requested the deaccessioning, seeks the best sale, auction, or exchange possibilities. All future sales of works of art for cash valued by the museum in excess of $5,000 will be at public auction, unless the proposed sale is to another museum or similar institution in which case consideration will be given to requests for extended times of payment.

3. Once a recommendation for sale or exchange is made, it is reviewed, modified as necessary, and approved in principle by the curator-in-chief (unless the curator-in-chief proposed the arrangement, in which case approval by the director is also required) and by the secretary.

4. After the proposal is approved in principle, the secretary reviews and approves the exact terms of the sale or exchange and, in the case of a consignment sale, such terms are then set forth in a letter agreement signed by the secretary on behalf of the museum.

In sum, this is a three-step process for objects of $25,000 or less: (1) notice to the attorney general, if required; (2) approval of the method of disposal and the price by the curator-in-chief (or the director, as appropriate) and by the secretary; and (3) approval by the secretary of the proper form of agreement. A copy of any executed agreement or memorandum of agreement is sent to the curator-in-chief and the treasurer.

Objects Valued Above $25,000

In regard to objects valued in excess of $25,000 which have been deaccessioned by the board of trustees or the Executive Committee:

1. Whenever it is proposed that the museum offer for exchange or sale to another museum, or for exchange to any third party, an object valued by the museum at more than $25,000, at least three disinterested outside appraisals will be obtained. In setting up the procedures for selecting such outside appraisers, the museum will solicit the views of knowledgeable third parties.

2. No object, valued by the museum at more than $25,000, and which has been on exhibition in the museum within the preced-

ing 10 years, will be disposed of until at least 45 days after the issue of a public notice identifying the work and giving the range of its estimated value based on outside appraisals. Copies of such notice will be available to museums, scholars and art historians who request them. At the conclusion of this 45-day period, public comments will be studied, and either the board or its Executive Committee will again consider the work in question and make the final decision. If the decision is to proceed, the following steps are taken.

3. The curator-in-chief, the director, or at their request, the curator in charge of the department which requested the deaccessioning, seeks the best sale or exchange possibilities.

4. Once a recommendation for sale or exchange is made, it is reviewed, modified as necessary, and approved in principle, by the curator-in-chief (unless the curator-in-chief proposed the arrangement, in which case approval by the director is also required) and by the secretary.

5. After such preliminary approval is obtained, a memorandum setting forth the proposal is prepared and approved in writing by the curator-in-chief and the secretary.

6. The memorandum is then submitted to the director and the president who signify their approval by signing the memorandum and returning it to the secretary for further action. Prior to the disposal, the museum obtains approval from the donor or his heirs if available. Where objections have been made the work has not been disposed of but has been reaccessioned and retained. This aspect of the procedure is applied to works valued below as well as above $25,000.

7. The president remains free to resubmit, and sometimes has resubmitted, the proposal to the members of the Acquisitions Committee.

8. The exact terms of the agreement are then prepared by the secretary who is also responsible for concluding the transaction. The transaction shall not be concluded until the terms of the sale or exchange have been approved by the Acquisitions Committee.

9. A copy of the final executed agreement is sent to the president, the director, the curator-in-chief, and the treasurer.

10. In all cases, irrespective of value, the sale or exchange of the object is reported to the next meeting of the board of trustees following receipt of all funds or the completion of the exchange.

11. The museum's annual report will include a statement of the cash proceeds from the sale of objects disposed of during the relevant year, and will describe each object sold or exchanged valued at more than $25,000.

Report to the Deaccessioning Task Force of the Registrars Committee of AAM

by Roberta Frey Gilboe

Review of the Current State of Practice for Deaccessioning

This review of current practices in museums concerning deaccessioning is based on a study of the deaccessioning policies and/or forms of 79 institutions that were submitted at the request of the Registrars Committee Deaccessioning Task Force. The object of the review is to provide readers with a sense of how museums that actively deaccession view the process and how they describe and define it in their policies. A more detailed breakdown of information about each of the museum types is attached at the end of this report, but, generally, the museums that submitted information concerning their deaccessioning policies can be divided into the following categories:

Art	29 (37%)
History	22 (28%)
Natural History/Anthropology	16 (20%)
General	12 (15%)

It is the intent of this review to provoke thought and discussion, and to encourage an assessment of the reader's own procedures rather than to necessarily draw hard and fast conclusions from the practices of other institutions. An effort is made to distinguish which types of museums use which elements of the process and which ones use elements of the process most frequently. Interesting phrases or concepts in policies are noted when they occur as well as instances in the policies that are unusual or stand out.

Roberta Frey Gilboe is associate registrar, Detroit Institute of Arts, and chair, Deaccession Task Force, Registrars Committee of AAM. This report was prepared in 1997.

The policies that were submitted represent the opinions of those institutions that have active deaccessioning programs, so the opinions of those that choose not to deaccession objects are not represented in this review of current practice. In many instances, the deaccession policies that were sent in, came with a note from the registrar or curator that their policies were currently under review or were in the process of being revised. Many contributors commented that they were looking forward to some discussion and guidance concerning the issue of deaccessioning objects in their collections, so this review of current practice may come at a timely moment for many institutions.

GENERAL ATTITUDES TOWARD DEACCESSIONING

A number of museums note in their policies that deaccessioning is a very serious step and warn that museum collections are a public trust and the first consideration in the deaccessioning process is the museum's responsibility to the public. Various policies emphasize that deaccessioning should be carefully considered and, when undertaken, should follow the established museum procedures strictly and be documented carefully. It is noted that errors in the deaccessioning process can lessen public confidence in the institution and can have an impact on the good will that the community and future donors feel toward the institution. One art museum begins its deaccession policy with the injunction, "the spirit of caution should inform the entire process of deaccessioning." Another art museum instructs staff that, "because of its complex legal and ethical nature, the deaccession process requires even greater deliberation than the acquisition of objects and will be handled in an open and candid manner."

For the purposes of the review, the process of deaccessioning is broken down into the following four sections:

I. Criteria for Deaccessioning

II. Procedures

III. Disposition

IV. Use of Proceeds

Each section will note how many institutions had elements of the deaccession process outlined in their policies and what types of institutions cited these elements, both by number and by percentages. *(Note: Percentage figures are rounded up; therefore, in some cases the totals add up to 99 or 101 percent. Also, where 10 or fewer policies discuss a particular element, the percentage figures are not broken down.)* As noted above, the contributing institutions have been broken into the categories of art, history (including historic buildings), natural history/anthropology, and general. General museums often have collections that have objects from all of the preceding categories and therefore can be interpreted to have concerns similar to any of the other institution categories. The National Park Service also contributed its deaccession policy to the task force and, though hard to categorize, is included in the general category.

I. CRITERIA FOR DEACCESSIONING

Deaccessioning is described in some policies as the act of removing an object from the accessioned collection of an institution. The deaccessioning process begins in most institutions when it is determined that the object meets one or more of the institution's deaccessioning criteria. Many policies list only a few or, in some cases, only one or two criteria to use to determine whether an object should be deaccessioned.

COLLECTIONS POLICY

1. The object does not fall within the scope of the collections criteria of the museum as defined in the accessions policy.

> 45 policies of 79 (57% of total) reviewed
> 16 Art. 36%
> 13 History. 29%
> 9 Natural History/Anthropology 20%
> 7 General 16%

Institutions often use very similar wording, and two art museums have this element as their only criteria, one noting that the object "no longer met the standards of the museum collection," and the other noting that the object is "not compatible with collection management criteria." Two institutions (art and history) include the comment that ancillary items, like frames, pedestals, etc., could be deaccessioned using this criteria.

2. The object is deemed irrelevant or no longer useful to the educational purposes of the museum.

> 32 policies: 41%
>
> 13 History 41%
>
> 7 Natural History/Anthropology 22%
>
> 7 General 22%
>
> 5 Art 16%

Three institutions use the wording that the object no longer furthers or serves the institution's "mission." Six institutions (two natural history/anthropology, four history) use the wording, "Doubtful potential for utilization in the foreseeable future."

3. Upgrading the quality of the collection.

> 12 policies: 15%
>
> 7 Art 58%
>
> 3 History 25%
>
> 1 General 8%
>
> 1 Natural History/Anthropology 8%

There is a wide range of interpretations for upgrading the collection and in a number of instances, this is the only criteria in the museum's policy that is to be considered when deaccessioning an object. A historic building considers the only deaccession criteria to be to "deaccession items in a manner which [provides] greatest possible benefit to the [institution]." A general museum asks, "Is the object or specimen occupying space and using valuable resources that could be better used to improve or strengthen another area of the collections in order to further the museum goals?" And a history museum asks, "Is there a need to improve or strengthen another area of the general history collection in order to further the goals of the institution?" These questions are open to interpretation and seem to indicate that the greater good of the collection may potentially be considered over the individual object's context and meaning.

Collection policies that define upgrading the quality of the collection more concretely, approach the idea from the point of view of the object. Two art museums note that works should be traded up for better examples. Another art museum will deaccession if the opportunity arises to acquire a better work by the same artist or by one within the same range. Yet another art museum states that deaccessioning is appropriate when a better and comparable example can be obtained through the exchange of the object in question.

One art museum does warn that, "great caution should be exercised to avoid disposing of works of art in one area of the collection purely for the motive of acquiring works in another area."

4. The object is determined to be significantly more useful and relevant to the collections and programs of another museum or educational institution than to those of the museum.

6 policies: 8%
3 History
2 Natural History/Anthropology
1 General

One university art museum notes that an object may be considered for deaccessioning if it would be more appropriately placed in another university department, i.e., the rare book library or the archive. A natural history/anthropology museum sees this criteria as providing an opportunity to "carry out mutually beneficial exchanges of materials with other museums or educational or scientific institutions."

5. Other collections policy issues

In the reviewed policies there are some additional comments that relate to other collections policy issues. Two art museums have the criteria, "works given to be sold." This is an acceptable criteria for deaccessioning, however, it may be noted that an institution should not formally accession an object given for resale, thus avoiding the deaccessioning process altogether. The National Park Service discusses this and advises that, "because of potential tax liabilities defined by the Internal Revenue Service, you should not accession museum objects with the intent to deaccession them later." One major art museum states in its policy that it "strongly discourages" the acceptance of gifts specifically for deaccession.

Two institutions, one general and another history, add as a deaccessioning criteria, the removal of the record for an object that was unintentionally accessioned twice. Since deaccessioning relates to the removal of the actual object from the collection, this does not seem a deaccession criteria as much as an error that needs to be documented. A registrar may consider simply documenting the error, linking the two numbers and moving on.

Surprisingly, one natural history/anthropology museum, notes that it is legitimate to respond to a request by relatives for family memorabilia in the institution's possession and, "if public interest can be served," a photocopy of the object is to be made and the original documents returned to the family.

REDUNDANCY

The object is a duplicate of other objects in the collection and the duplication does not improve the collection.

    42 policies: 53 %
    18 Art. . . . . 43 %
    15 History. . . . . 36 %
    6 General . . . . 14 %
    3 Natural History/Anthropology . . . . 7 %

The wording throughout the policies concerning redundancy is very similar. Various art museum policies include the phrases, "redundant," "inferior duplicate," "similar but superior example," "exact duplicate," and "better and comparable example in collection." One art museum comments that duplication can include objects that have similar themes in a similar medium.

CONDITION OF THE OBJECT

1. The object is in such poor physical condition that proper restoration is not feasible, or would render the object essentially false.

    54 policies: 68 %
    22 Art. . . . . 41 %
    16 History. . . . . 30 %
    9 Natural History/Anthropology . . . . . . 17 %
    7 General . . . . 13 %

One art museum policy mentions "infested" as a deaccession criteria.

2. The object is found to be falsely attributed or documented or proved to be a fake or forgery.

29 policies: 37 %
```
14 Art........................... 48 %
6 Natural History/Anthropology ...... 21 %
6 History.......................... 21 %
3 General ........................ 10 %
```
3. The institution cannot care for the object properly.
25 policies: 32 %
```
8 History.......................... 32 %
7 General ........................ 28 %
7 Art............................ 28 %
3 Natural History/Anthropology ...... 12 %
```
Among the reasons cited as making it difficult to care properly for an object are that the cost is too great (history museum), undue size (natural history/anthropology), that the object cannot be displayed properly due to the limitations of the physical plant (art), and that it poses a threat to public safety if displayed in the manner prescribed by its design (art).

One art museum cites as a criteria that there is "no longer space to retain all objects." A natural history/anthropology museum will accept this as a criteria, but only "if the museum can designate another institution capable of fulfilling those obligations to the object."

4. The object is not aesthetically of museum quality and is not likely to ever be exhibited or loaned to other institutions.
19 policies: 24 %
```
13 Art........................... 68 %
4 General ........................ 21 %
1 History.......................... 5 %
1 Natural History/Anthropology ....... 5 %
```
One natural history/anthropology museum states that an object of poorer quality "that hinders the upgrading of collections and occupies valuable storage space" may be deaccessioned. A university art museum uses this criteria to determine that an object would be "better utilized by the college for comparative and study purposes."

One art museum discusses the possibility that an institution could make a "mistake" when collecting (only one) but also warns that changing tastes can complicate questions of quality and recommends backing up curatorial opinion with outside expertise to confirm deaccessioning decisions based on issues of aesthetic quality.

5. The object poses a hazard to human life or health or to other objects in the museum's collection.

> 13 policies: 16 %
> 5 History. . . . . 38 %
> 4 Natural History/Anthropology . . . . . . 31 %
> 4 General . . . . 31 %

No art museum policies reviewed noted this as a criteria for deaccessioning.

6. The object has been stolen or has been missing for more than two or three years.

> 11 policies: 14 %
> 7 History. . . . . 64 %
> 2 Natural History/Anthropology . . . . . . 18 %
> 2 General . . . . 18 %

Two institutions (history and natural history/anthropology) noted that this criteria applied when an institution sought to "negotiate insurance compensation for lost or stolen material." There is no explanation of the actual circumstances where this may occur; it may apply if an insurance company requests that the museum transfer the title of the stolen material when it compensates the museum for the loss. Many insurance policies feature a "buy-back clause" that allows the museum to recover the item and take possession from the insurance company if the item is recovered and title would transfer again back to the museum.

An institution may wish to think twice about deaccessioning a stolen object if the insurance company is not insisting on the title transfer. If the object is recovered what will be the ramifications of the institution having deaccessioned it? If it is in someone else's possession, the museum may need to prove that it diligently attempted to recover the object. Deaccessioning seems to indicate a lack of "due diligence" sometimes required by the courts when attempting to retrieve the object from a new owner.

Again, deaccessioning is the act of removing the object from the institution's collection. If theft has already removed the object, is it wise to use the deaccession process to clean up the paperwork?

OWNERSHIP

1. The object is determined to have been acquired in a manner contrary to the museum's acquisitions policy, i.e., the work may have been determined to be stolen or illegally exported or imported in violation of applicable state and federal laws.

> 10 policies: 13 %
> 6 Art
> 2 General
> 1 History
> 1 Natural History/Anthropology

One institution comments that the means of disposal will be determined on a case by case basis.

2. The object has been determined to rightfully belong to a group or individual other than the museum.

> 4 policies: 5 %
> 3 General
> 1 History

One art museum that added the criteria that an object may be considered for deaccessioning if it is found to be a portion of a whole, of which other parts belong to another institution.

COMPLIANCE WITH INTERNATIONAL, FEDERAL AND STATE LAW

The object is subject to compliance with federal and state legislation and regulations, i.e., UNESCO conventions or the reburial of human remains and associated funerary objects and the repatriation of sacred objects and items of cultural patrimony.

> 10 policies: 13 %
> 4 Natural History/Anthropology
> 3 Art
> 2 General
> 1 History

Three institutions (history, natural history/anthropology and general) mentioned compliance with NAGPRA legislation specifically. Three art museums mentioned compliance with UNESCO conventions specifically.

Two institutions (art and general) note that for the purposes of repatriation, when it can be shown that other bodies or governments have a right to the material, "the museum will proceed with repatriation only when it has assurances that the object will be preserved in accordance with the highest standards of the museum profession."

One history policy notes that, "items which may be the subject of future demands for repatriation should not be subject to deaccessioning. The museum has a moral obligation to protect materials that may be considered sacred or a part of a nation's cultural heritage."

HISTORY, NATURAL HISTORY, AND ANTHROPOLOGY MUSEUM CONSIDERATIONS

1. The object is to be subjected to destructive analysis when the information expected to be obtained is judged to outweigh the value of the specimen and its possible future use. Objects that are particularly numerous will be considered as especially suitable.

> 8 policies: 10 %
> 5 Natural History/Anthropology
> 1 Art
> 1 History
> 1 General

2. The object lacks history or provenance.

> 7 policies: 9 %
> 5 Natural History/Anthropology
> 1 History
> 1 General

Provenance is a particularly important issue for natural history and anthropology museums that collect many specimens. One natural history/anthropology museum notes that specimens with substandard documentation, which lack information about the collector, time and place collected, may have no value for research and may simply waste space and staff time.

An additional consideration is mentioned by two institutions, one general and one natural history/anthropology. If an object has a ritual use or sacred nature and appropriate care is not possible in the museum environment this can be used as a deaccession criteria.

20TH-CENTURY ART COLLECTIONS CONSIDERATIONS

Deaccessioning the work of a living artist.
    5 policies: 6 % (all from art museums)

Two art museums state unequivocally that no work of a living artist should be deaccessioned except to replace it with a stronger work by the same artist. They direct that the artist should be consulted. Another strongly discourages the practice, except to upgrade, and again urges that the artist be contacted.

Another museum allows the deaccessioning of work by living artists, with no requirement that the museum acquire another of the same artist's work. This institution suggests that consideration be given to notifying the artist.

Finally, a museum that is open to deaccessioning the works of living artists suggests that any applicable legal or contractual restriction on the disposition should be determined and observed.

II. PROCEDURES

DEACCESSIONING APPROVAL PROCESS

The *Museum Handbook* published by the National Park Service features a chapter on deaccessioning that includes the comment that the best deaccession policy is a good accession policy. For many institutions, the deaccessioning process mirrors the accessioning process with the object recommended for deaccessioning going through the same approval processes and governing board reviews that an object recommended for accessioning would go through. Since every institution has a slightly different structure and different names for governing boards and committees that are consulted in the process of reviewing objects, this review of practice will not try to compare the exact process in every museum, but will review the procedures that are common to many institutions. Some of the policies carefully documented every step in the approval process and, in general, that thoroughness in documenting procedures is to be highly recommended.

One major art museum's policy recommends that the deliberations required by the deaccessioning process be carried out "in an orderly and thorough fashion, without undue speed and over a period of time." Two museums specify in their procedures that a waiting period is required when deaccessioning an object. A general museum recommends that the process take a minimum of a year in order to insure that the process is correct and protects the integrity of the museum. An art museum requires a six-month waiting period after all the documentation has been accumulated and reviewed. After six months the deaccession package will be reviewed again before deaccessioning can proceed.

When the museum's procedures for deaccessioning are followed and completed, when the object has been reviewed by the appropriate committees and boards and all the necessary approvals have been obtained, in accordance with the museum's policies, the object may be considered to be officially removed from the collection of the museum.

INITIATING DEACCESSIONING

56 policies: 71 %
18 Art. . . . . 32 %
16 History. . . . . 29 %
11 General . . . . 20 %
11 Natural History/Anthropology . . . . . 20 %

These 56 policies discuss to some degree or another where the process of deaccessioning should begin. With only rare exceptions, the policies are very much in agreement that it is the curator responsible for the object, the collections management team or the registrar who are to recommend an object for deaccessioning. In a few instances a director is empowered to recommend deaccessioning and in one instance, a history museum notes that a member of the board of trustees can recommend that an object be considered for deaccessioning. One general institution requires that it be noted during the process that the proposal originated with the curator and not with the governing board or the director.

A major art museum notes that the standard procedure is for the curator to recommend deaccessioning, but the director and the board of trustees can also recommend "in the event of the dissolution or radical change in the function or structure of the department." Another art museum comments that if any member of the staff objects to the deaccessioning of the object, it will remain in the collection. A natural history/anthropology museum comments that artifacts will be disposed of contrary to the advice of professional staff "only for clear and compelling reasons."

WRITTEN DOCUMENTATION REQUIRED

    32 policies: 41 %

    16 Art. . . . . 50 %

    9 History. . . . . 28 %

    4 Natural History/Anthropology . . . . . . 13 %

    3 General . . . . 9 %

There are 32 policies that mention that some written documentation is required, although not all of them outline what information they expect to be in the recommendation. Fourteen policies include a sample of the internal forms that they require to be filled out when deaccessioning. Those policies that do describe the information that they require, include the reason for deaccessioning as well as the donor, the object's history and provenance, its significance, physical condition, an appraisal, the proposed method of disposal, and request that a photograph be included. While many policies may not state that the recommendation is to be made in writing, a close reading of the procedures implies that some degree of written documentation is required.

INDEPENDENT APPRAISALS

    23 policies: 29 %

    13 Art. . . . . 57 %

    5 Natural History/Anthropology . . . . . . 22 %

    3 General . . . . 13 %

    2 History. . . . . 9 %

The policies discuss the circumstances that would require an outside appraisal and their requirements are wide-ranging. Usually an outside appraisal is provided to establish market value or to confirm a high value item.

Art museums tend to deal in high-value objects and often require appraisals when an object is judged to be valued above $5,000. One art museum policy states that one independent appraisal is required if the value of the object is less than $5,000; two are required if it is over $5,000; three if it is over $50,000. Another art museum requires two independent appraisals if the object is valued above $25,000.

Natural history/anthropology and history policies tend to work with objects of lower value but are no less concerned with securing appraisals for collections and specimens, especially when they are being considered for sale. Two natural history/anthropology policies recommend outside appraisals when the fair market value is estimated to be more than $750 for an individual specimen or $5,000 for a collection.

In the context of an exchange, one large institution comments that appraisals are a necessary and accepted museum practice when conducting an exchange to ensure that an exchange is creditable and equitable, to maintain the public trust, to avoid any conflict of interest or even the appearance of a conflict of interest.

EXPERT OPINIONS

       13 policies: 16 %
       10 Art............................ 77 %
       2 History......................... 15 %
       1 General .... 8 %

In addition to appraisals, a few museums, primarily art museums, consider consulting outside experts under some circumstances. Three museums affiliated with universities suggest consulting a member of the faculty for an opinion.

When objects are being deaccessioned using quality as a criteria, one art museum notes that "changing taste complicates questions about quality" and outside expertise should be sought to confirm the institution's judgment in deaccessioning decisions. Only two art museum policies require that an outside expert be consulted. Otherwise the policies use the language, "if necessary" and "when appropriate."

CONSERVATION REPORTS

Conservation reports are something of an afterthought. Three art museum policies mention them specifically, one if the object is valued above $15,000; one that states that objects being considered for deaccession because of their deteriorated condition require a report from a conservation specialist; and one that requires both an appraisal and a conservation report to proceed with deaccessioning.

LEGAL REQUIREMENTS

> 9 policies: 11%
> 4 Art
> 2 History
> 2 Natural History/Anthropology
> 1 General

A major art museum includes the comment in its policy that objects must be deaccessioned strictly in accordance with legal requirements and notes that legal compliance will be the responsibility of the museum registrar. The registrar is to seek legal counsel to assure full compliance with any legal requirements. This is the only policy that places this responsibility in the hands of the registrar.

Two policies (natural history/anthropology and history) state that there will be no transaction that violates state or federal laws or violates institution's policies. A history policy states that governmental regulations shall be observed. An art policy states that staff must comply with all applicable local, state and U.S. federal laws in force at the time.

TITLE

1. Review the object's accession records and all other pertinent documentation to insure the museum holds valid title to the object.

> 41 policies: 52%
> 15 Art 37%
> 12 History. 29%
> 8 Natural History/Anthropology 20%
> 6 General 15%

Most of the policies state explicitly that it must be determined that the museum holds clear legal title to the object; however, some policies are less specific. Six policies (one natural history/anthropology, one general, one art, three history) use similar wording to the effect that reasonable efforts will be made to ascertain that the museum has a legal right to deaccession. One history policy only requires that it be determined that the institution "is free to do so [deaccession]." One art museum instructs staff to "determine whether any legal or precatory restrictions are attached to the object in question."

In the event that there are questions about title, one history policy states that the staff will present all information to the board of trustees, which will resolve the issue on a case by case basis. Another history policy states that proof of ownership is not required to deaccession items that have negligible market value.

2. Abandoned property
    5 policies: 6 %
    3 History
    1 General
    1 Art

Many museums have objects in their collections that meet the criteria for deaccessioning, but to which they do not have legal title. In some states legislation has been passed that outlines a process that a museum must follow in order to acquire title to objects that have been on the premises for a long period of time without title having been established, but each institution must refer to its own state's laws and regulations concerning abandoned property.

One general museum outlined the process it follows when title cannot be established using the museum's records. Legislation concerning abandoned property has been established in the museum's state, and it performs the following procedures to comply with the law:

> The item is carefully catalogued. A notice is placed in the newspaper stating that the museum intends to dispose of certain objects and if anyone has an ownership interest in these objects, they need to come to the museum within six months with proof of their claim. Objects that are not claimed will be disposed of. After six months, items under $500 may be sold, items over

$500 can be sold after the attorney has cleared title through a court action. The policy states that the museum must follow these procedures and establish title before deaccessioning an object. It is not acceptable to deaccession an object without first establishing title.

A college art museum in another state directs that if the source of the object is unknown and the records do not indicate possession by the college for more than 25 years, the (state's) Unclaimed Property Law should be followed. Objects that have not been claimed in 25 years may be considered the college's property as of Jan. 1, 1985, pursuant to state law (which is cited in the policy).

One history policy notes that loaned objects are deaccessioned as abandoned property upon the approval of the board of trustees and legal counsel. Another history policy notes that "the board has the authority to deaccession . . . material that the society owns by default under state abandoned property laws and material that is found in the collections without records or accession numbers."

3. *Term of possession*
> 5 policies: 6 %
> 2 History
> 1 Natural History/Anthropology
> 1 Art
> 1 General

A few institutions note that the object must have been in the collection for a minimum period of time before it can be deaccessioned. Two policies (art and history) require three years. A natural history/anthropology policy requires five years (unless the object poses a danger). Two policies (general and history) require two years and the history policy directs staff to see the U.S. Tax Reform Act of 1984 and IRS regulations.

DONOR-IMPOSED RESTRICTIONS
> 28 policies: 35 %
> 9 History. . . . . 32 %
> 7 General . . . . 25 %
> 6 Art. . . . . 21 %
> 6 Natural History/Anthropology . . . . . . 21 %

These policies have comments about observing, to some degree, restrictions imposed by donors when the object was originally accessioned. Nine of the policies (three general, one history, one natural history/anthropology, four art) state that the wishes of the donor are to be respected. One history museum states that there is to be no deaccessioning of objects "when such action is counter to any written agreements between the society and the donor." An art museum directs the staff to "respect the clearly expressed wishes of the donors, whether mandatory or precatory, as stated in correspondence, deed of gift, or will."

Some policies give themselves some latitude in their approach to donor-imposed restrictions. Two policies (history and general) state that "reasonable efforts" are to be made to comply with restricting conditions. A history policy states that mandatory restrictions are to be observed until the donors or their heirs can be consulted. A natural history/anthropology policy states that original restrictions or requests "will be considered."

One major art museum states that mandatory restrictions are to be strictly observed, but while precatory requests (i.e., non-binding preferences of donors) should be taken into account where possible, such requests do not need to be followed if it is not in the best interests of the institution. Three natural history/anthropology and four history policies state that mandatory restrictions are to be observed "unless deviation from their terms is authorized by a court of competent jurisdiction."

If adherence to mandatory or precatory restrictions is impossible or detrimental to the museum or if there are questions concerning the intent or force of the restrictions, legal counsel may be asked to evaluate the possibility of removing the restrictions.

     20 policies: 25 %
     8 History. . . . . 40 %
     6 Art. . . . . 30 %
     4 General . . . . 20 %
     2 Natural History/Anthropology . . . . . . 10 %

The policies for one general, three natural history/anthropology, and five history institutions advise that if there are questions concerning the intent or force of the restrictions, the museum should seek legal advice. The policies for two art museums comment that restrictions are to be observed unless it can be clearly shown that adherence to such restrictions is impossible or substantially detrimental to the museum and add that the museum can only be relieved from such restrictions through appropriate legal procedures. A history museum notes that "restrictions will be considered prior to deaccessioning," and "reserves the right to take appropriate legal action to remove such conditions."

DONOR NOTIFICATION

When the object was accessioned as a gift or bequest, reasonable efforts will be made to locate the donors or heirs of the original donors to notify them of the intended deaccession.

       29 policies: 37%
       16 Art 55%
       7 History 24%
       4 General 14%
       2 Natural History/Anthropology 7%

These 29 policies agree that, to some extent, the museum has an obligation to make a reasonable attempt to notify the original donor or heirs. Five policies (three art, one natural history/anthropology, and one history) state that it is a matter of courtesy to notify the donor. Three art museums add that the notification of the donor is not to be construed as a request for permission to deaccession.

One art policy states that if the donor objects to the deaccession, the director, in consultation with the curator, will decide whether to proceed. A general museum remarks that an extremely negative reaction from the donor may be considered a valid reason to reconsider the deaccessioning process.

Only one policy reviewed, an art museum (not included in the above statistics), states in its policy that it does not require that the original donors be notified.

CREDIT LINE

The original donor shall receive credit on exhibit labels, in publications, and in the museum's records for objects purchased with the proceeds from the sale of the deaccessioned object.

> 18 policies: 23%
>
> 13 Art............................. 72%
> 2 General 11%
> 2 History........................... 11%
> 1 Natural History/Anthropology 6%

DOCUMENTATION

All information concerning the deaccessioned object is maintained in a permanent file.

> 48 policies: 61%
>
> 18 Art............................. 38%
> 13 History........................... 27%
> 9 Natural History/Anthropology 19%
> 8 General 17%

Most policies are rather general about what information needs to be kept, but some are more specific, and include all the information pertinent to the deaccessioning process as part of the permanent record. Some of the policies specify that the registrar and/or the curator are responsible for maintaining the permanent file. One history policy suggests that a reasonable effort be made to keep a record of the location of deaccessioned objects after they are released from the collection. An art museum also suggests tracking the object, "to aid researchers."

PUBLIC DISCLOSURE

> 10 policies: 13%
> 6 Art
> 3 History
> 1 General

Few policies mention public disclosure of the process and those that do, vary to a certain extent in their approach. One general museum requires that the deaccessioning program be publicized in ways that are likely to attract public approval and support. The policy states that no attempt will be made to minimize the importance of the program or hide it from public notice, commenting that deaccession records are public records.

Other institutions that are equally open about the process include an art museum that comments that the object file is a permanent public record to be maintained and made available by the museum. Another art museum requires that each step be carefully documented and the minutes of the curatorial and board meetings are to record deaccessioning information. Most institutions note that the deaccessioning process normally proceeds through a variety of meetings and board reviews; few policies mention (but may assume it is obvious) that the minutes of these meetings would note the deaccessioned items.

A number of policies note that they will provide deaccessioning information to the public on request, although two policies (both history) noted that they would provide information in reply to a "responsible request."

III. DISPOSITION

A natural history/anthropology policy defines the disposition of the deaccessioned object as "the actual transaction by which museum objects are removed permanently from the premises of the museum."

GUIDELINES

The manner of disposition should be in the best interests of the museum, the public it serves, the public trust it represents and the scholarly and cultural communities it serves.

> 14 policies: 18%
> 7 History. 50%
> 3 Art. 21%
> 2 General 14%
> 2 Natural History/Anthropology 14%

When discussing disposition, a number of policies make comments concerning the process. An art museum advises that "the most open method of disposal is strongly encouraged. Any appearance of impropriety or favoritism must be avoided." Another institution recommends choosing the option that will offer the greatest ability to care for the objects, ability to preserve the objects in the public sector, and/or the greatest likelihood for public benefit.

A very large general museum greatly discourages sale or exchange of objects with individuals, non-cultural or non-scholarly entities. On the other hand, two art museums instruct that disposition decisions are to be made to the "maximum advantage of the [museum's] collections.

DISPOSITION DETERMINED BY

```
27 policies:  34%
13 Art........................... 48%
7 History......................... 26%
4 General ........................ 15%
3 Natural History/Anthropology ...... 11%
```

The majority of the policies that discuss disposition recommend that the curator, staff collections team, and/or director are to make the decision concerning how the object is to be disposed. Often it is recommended that the plan of disposition accompany the original recommendation for deaccessioning when deaccessioning the object is first proposed. The plan of disposition requires the approval of the board of trustees or governing boards in many cases.

One general policy states that the "current market value will determine the method of final disposition." A history policy instructs that items less than $2,500 may be disposed of in a reasonable manner and those over $2,500 will be appraised and sold at public auction.

DISPOSITION TO OTHER INSTITUTIONS

1. First preference will be given to other institutions.
```
28 policies: 35%
9 History......................... 32%
9 Natural History/Anthropology ...... 32%
6 General ........................ 21%
4 Art............................. 14%
```

These policies discuss the idea that preference may be given to placing objects in another nonprofit institution. An art museum notes that in disposing of objects, first consideration is to be given to the museum community at large. The policy comments that sales to, or exchanges between, museums reinforce those institutions' roles as custodians of the public trust and are to receive priority.

A number of institutions use similar wording, stating that preference will be given to placing the object in another public institution through transfer, exchange, or sale where it can serve the purpose for which it was originally acquired. One history policy includes a loan of deaccessioned material to another institution as an option. Another history policy comments that when deaccessioned materials are of primary research value and are still in useful condition, the institution is to make every effort to place them in an institution where they will be accessible to researchers.

The policy for a natural history/anthropology museum outlined a process that only disposes of objects to other institutions. Another natural history/anthropology museum states that the exchange of artifacts with a similar institution is the most desirable means of disposal, commenting that such exchanges increase the likelihood that the object will be preserved and kept within the public domain.

2. Placing the object in another institution will be considered as a disposition alternative.

> 15 policies: 19 %
> 7 Art. . . . . 47 %
> 4 History. . . . . 27 %
> 2 Natural History/Anthropology . . . . . . 13 %
> 2 General . . . . 13 %

These policies suggest that consideration be given to other institutions, often using the wording "where appropriate." The policies for five art museums and one general museum noted that one avenue is to dispose of objects to other institutions by gift, sale, or exchange but they did not promote this as a particular preference.

3. Other disposition comments concerning other institutions.

One art policy comments that no item of significance to the state is to be sold or traded outside of the state without review by the collections committee. A history policy mentions a geographic preference, commenting that it would give preference to options that place the object within the most appropriate geographic region.

DISPOSITION METHODS

1. Transfers/Gifts

A natural history/anthropology policy defines a transfer as "the conveyance of ownership of a museum object without remuneration." Another natural history/anthropology museum defines it as the "permanent removal from the [museum's] collections and placement in another institution or organization without reciprocal compensation."

    57 policies: 72%
    17 Art 30%
    14 History 25%
    13 Natural History/Anthropology 23%
    13 General 23%

These 57 policies make some mention of the use of gift or transfer as a means of disposing of an object. Of these policies, 38 note that a transfer is to be used to place an object in another institution, and several remark that a transfer or gift is never to be used as a means of disposing of an object to an individual or for-profit entity.

The policies for two natural history/anthropology museums comment that it is customary in some disciplines for scientists who borrow and identify biological or paleontological specimens to retain some duplicate examples for the collections of their institution. Such gifts of specimens usually involve negligible monetary value. They direct that all such transactions are to be in keeping with the norms of the scientific discipline involved. Another natural history/anthropology museum mentions that "in certain disciplines (i.e., mineralogy), trading of specimens is [an] available method of increasing the [institution's] holdings."

The policies for two art museums authorize the "transfer a work of art in their collections to another public or nonprofit institution when the transfer is in the public interest." They note three criteria for a transfer, requiring that the object have more significance to the other institution; that the social, cultural, or historical value of the work outweighs its monetary value; and that the work of art is more likely to be preserved and available to the public in the receiving institution.

One general museum allows transfers when the value of the work is nominal and a natural history/anthropology policy notes that a transfer is to be used only to place an object with another institution and only when a sale or exchange is not possible.

2. Exchange

A natural history/anthropology policy defines an exchange as "the conveyance of ownership of a museum object in return for title to an object from another institution." Another natural history/anthropology museum says that exchanges serve to "advance the research, education and exhibition programs of all parties." One last natural history/anthropology policy defines an exchange as the "roughly reciprocal movement of objects between the [museum's] collections and those of an outside institution or individual."

> 62 policies: 78 %
> 23 Art. . . . . 37 %
> 14 Natural History/Anthropology . . . . . 23 %
> 14 History. . . . . 23 %
> 11 General . . . . 18 %

There are 62 policies that make some mention of the use of an exchange as a means of disposing of an object and 31 of the policies indicate a preference for exchanging objects with other institutions. The policies for three institutions (one history and two natural history/anthropology) specifically state that they are not to exchange objects with individuals or for-profit entities; however, six other institutions (four art, one general and one history) state that they see no difficulties making an exchange with an artist, a reputable dealer, or a collector. It is noted in a number of policies that if the deaccessioned object is exchanged for another work, the general requirement for acquisitions must be followed as well as for deaccessions.

One very large general institution notes that methods vary with the specimen in question. For example, a long-term open exchange (the giving of a specimen with the expectation that sometime in the future a comparable specimen may be given in return) is appropriate for scientific specimens of little commercial value. Such a method is inappropriate if the specimen is valuable or the recipient is a commercial entity. Preferably, exchanges are to be made with scholarly and cultural organizations.

A natural history/anthropology policy comments that the formal reciprocal transfer of material or specimens between two or more institutions, or between an institution and an individual, is desirable if it serves to advance the research, educational, or exhibition programs of both parties. Generally, the policy states, exchanges are not made unless the material has been studied, determined, documented, or represents duplicate or out-of-scope material.

One art museum policy cautions that when anything other than a public auction is used to dispose of an object, the museum must obtain three independent estimates of fair market value or three bids. A natural history/anthropology policy directs the museum never to exchange archaeological material and portions of the paleontological and biological collections with an individual or for-profit entity.

3. Sale

Using a sale as a method of disposition evokes very different responses from museums. Most policies are favorable toward using a sale as a disposition method, although some require certain conditions to be met before an object is to be placed in a sale. Several policies expressed reservations about sales; one natural history/anthropology policy notes that the decision to dispose of specimens through sale should be carefully considered and is discouraged. Two policies (natural history/anthropology and history) state that only if the object is inappropriate for gift or exchange with another institution, or cannot be placed in an education department, can consideration then be given to offering the object for sale at a public auction.

    a. Public sale/auction
      56 policies: 71%
      25 Art. 45%
      13 History. 23%

10 Natural History/Anthropology . . . . . 18 %

8 General . . . . 14 %

These 56 policies make some mention of the use of a public sale or auction as a means of disposing of an object. There are a variety of approaches to the idea of using a public sale to dispose of deaccessioned objects. The policies for five institutions (three natural history/anthropology, one history, one general) suggest using a sale as a last resort, only if the object cannot be placed in another nonprofit organization. The policies for eight institutions (three history, four art, one history) mention specifically that a public sale is the preferred method of disposition.

The policy for a major art museum comments that sale at public auction is strongly encouraged and another art museum directs that all sales will be conducted openly by the seller at public auction. Yet another large art museum states that, unless otherwise decided, all dispositions shall be by public sale and the primary objective shall be to obtain the best possible price for the object being sold.

Many policies comment that the openness of public sales and auctions is preferred to private sales, although one general museum preferred that the sale of deaccessioned objects be through a "discreet auction," which is not entirely clear but may mean that the museum wishes to remain anonymous at a public auction. A history policy states that a public sale is the only means by which an individual can acquire a deaccessioned object.

b. Private/direct sale

36 policies: 46 %

16 Art . . . . 44 %

7 General . . . . 19 %

7 Natural History/Anthropology . . . . . . 19 %

6 History . . . . 17 %

Thirty-five policies make some mention of a private or direct sale as a means of disposition. Of these policies, seven (two general, one art, three natural history/anthropology, one history) prefer that private sales only be arranged with other institutions; a natural history/anthropology policy states that no privately arranged sales may be made "except to other museums or educational or scientific institutions."

An art museum finds private sales acceptable only if the object fails to sell publicly. Two policies (art and general) direct that when anything other than a public auction is used to dispose of an object, the museum must obtain three independent estimates of fair market value or three bids. A natural history/anthropology policy okays private sales when the deaccessioned objects have been given widespread publicity with particular attention aimed at the appropriate audience of potential buyers.

Several policies voice strong concerns about selling privately to individuals and a history policy specifically states that in no case will objects be given or sold privately to an individual. The policy also states that it will sell an object privately after competitive bids have been placed by established dealers. Also the museum may sell to another institution if there are two independent appraisals and the recipient intends to use the object to further its mission.

Finally, one natural history/anthropology policy states that the museum will ensure that it never sells objects for less than fair market value. The policy also mentions that the museum will sell objects to a nonprofit institution in preference to an individual or for profit institution, "all other factors being equal."

   c. Sale method not specified
      9 policies: 11 %
      4 History
      3 Art
      1 Natural History/Anthropology
      1 General

These nine policies mention sale as a method of disposition but do not specify the method. A natural history/anthropology policy states that the sale "must be in a manner that will best protect the interests, objectives, and legal status of the museum and adhere to the highest ethical standards." A history policy states that "all sales shall assure the public equal opportunity to purchase."

The natural history/anthropology policy directs that any method of sale "must be in a manner that will best protect the interests, objectives, and legal status of the museum and adhere to the highest ethical standards."

d. Using the museum shop to sell deaccessioned objects

The policies for five institutions (two natural history/anthropology, one history, one art, one general) state that deaccessioned objects are not to be sold through the shop or in any other form of sale on the museum's premises.

The policies for three natural history/anthropology policies state that, under certain circumstances, it is appropriate to sell deaccessioned objects through the museum shop. The policies state that if the object is inappropriate for inclusion in a teaching collection and of insufficient value for public auction, consideration will be given to selling the object through the museum shop.

One natural history/anthropology policy, which forbids the sale of deaccessioned objects through the shop, does comment that specimens culled from field collections, if they have never been accessioned, may be sold through the museum shop.

e. Museum identification at sale
    8 policies: 6%
    5 Art
    2 History
    1 General

The policies for four museums (three art and one general) state that the standard procedure is for the museum to always identify itself and suggests wording in the auction catalogue or sales literature along the following lines, "Property from [museum name], sold to benefit the acquisition fund" or "Sold by order of the board of trustees of [museum name]."

An art museum states that it "will not be identified as the owner of materials placed at auction." A history policy directs that the sale will be as discreet as possible, through a second party, and the museum will not be named in connection with the object.

Two policies (art and history) both state that the institution may identify itself, but "if there are compelling reasons, [deaccessioned objects] may be disposed of anonymously."

In addition to the eight policies that note their preferences for identification, a number of institutions of all types use the wording, concerning sales at public auction, that the objects must be advertised in a manner that, "will best protect the interests, objectives, and legal status of the museum."

f. Identification of the object

The policies for three art museums and one general museum require that all identifying information and labels be removed from the object, unless removal would cause damage. On the other hand, one large art museum requires that identifying numbers remain on the object and, if necessary, identifying numbers are painted on before it leaves the museum premises.

g. Sale of archaeological material

The policies for five natural history/anthropology museums express a concern about the sale of archaeological material. One states that no prehistoric material or material from any archaeological context, prehistoric or historic, shall be sold. Two note that archaeological objects will not be sold, in compliance with federal regulations. Two policies also note that vertebrate fossils will not be sold. One other institution states that objects in the archaeological, paleontological and biological collections are never to be sold.

4. Retain for educational or study purposes

17 policies: 22 %
5 Natural History/Anthropology . . . . . . 29 %
4 Art. . . . . 24 %
4 General . . . . 24 %
4 History. . . . . 24 %

These 17 policies suggest that consideration be given to transferring a deaccessioned object to an education department or study collection. Often the criteria cited for this kind of transfer is that the object is of minimal value or other institutions are not interested in acquiring the object. One general museum states that if objects are

damaged or deteriorated to the point of not being useful for disposal by other means, they may be given to appropriate educational
institutions for use in teaching activities (which did not strike the
reviewer as kind).

Other museums took a more altruistic view, one history museum
states that consideration will "first" be given to the museum's education collections for use as instructional aids or exhibit materials. A natural history/anthropology museum directs that specimens retaining
value for exhibition or educational purposes should be offered to the
appropriate department.

5. Destruction/Disposal
    46 policies: 58%
    14 Natural History/Anthropology 30%
    11 Art 24%
    11 History 24%
    10 General 22%

When determining whether to destroy an object, museums primarily
look at the condition of the object and whether it is hazardous. The
majority of policies reviewed agreed that destruction is appropriate
when the object is in a seriously deteriorated condition or is a hazard
to people or other objects.

A reason put forward in 11 policies (seven natural history/anthro-
pology, one art, two history, one general) states that the object may be
disposed of when no other alternatives exist. These policies comment
that if the object is without scientific value, of minimal market value,
unsuitable for transfer or trade, "devoid of museum appropriateness,"
etc.

One natural history/anthropology policy states that physical disposal or destruction of a deaccessioned object must be witnessed and
a record of the date and manner of disposal or destruction and witness
names must be on file with the registrar.

6. Repatriation/Reburial

A natural history/anthropology museum uses the following definition
in its policy: "The terms repatriation and reburial describe the return
for reinterment of human remains and/or other collections material to

the appropriate representatives of groups with a clear connection to the original group."

    9 policies: 11 %
    4 Natural History/Anthropology
    2 General
    1 Art
    1 History

The policies that discuss repatriation and/or reburial as a means of disposing of objects are usually referring to the NAGPRA legislation, and all are in agreement that they will abide by the terms of the legislation. Concerning this legislation, one natural history/anthropology policy states: "The museum abides by the letter and spirit of the NAGPRA and the [state's] Antiquities Act. Repatriation decisions will be undertaken on a case by case basis, in accordance with the museum's legal, fiduciarial and ethical responsibilities. The Indian Advisory Committee and the university's legal counsel office will consult in reburial/repatriation decisions."

One natural history/anthropology museum does state that it has a special concern for whether the material requested would be preserved and made accessible, if, when a repatriation claim is made, there are concerns about the material being lost to scholarly and public access, the most rigorous of standards will be applied before releasing it.

Only one policy, a general museum, discussed the issue of reburial in detail, but it did it very comprehensively and that section of the policy is quoted as follows:

Disposal of Native American human remains is regulated by the Native American Graves Protection Act of 1990.

1. If tribal or area affiliations are known, the remains will be turned over to the tribal or area governing body for funerary disposal as considered proper by the governing body.

2. If there is no tribal or area designation known, the nearest tribal governing body will be asked to accept responsibility for the remains and to arrange for proper funerary disposal.

3. If there is no one to accept responsibility for the remains they will be disposed of in one of the following ways at the

discretion of the institution involved and the Museum Collections Advisory Committee:

Release to an education institution which has an active program in physical anthropology or medical research with the final intent for disposition being the internment of the remains after an agreed upon period of study.

Internment in sanctioned ground at [state] expense.

7. Return to donor

    12 policies: 15%

    6 History. 50%

    3 Natural History/Anthropology 25%

    2 General 17%

    1 Art. 8%

Of the 12 policies, three (natural history/anthropology, history, general) state that no deaccessioned objects are to be returned to the original donor(s). The history museum policy states that no item deaccessioned will be returned to the original donor or the donor's heirs, both because of the uncertainty of which family member would be entitled to the object, and because the IRS forbids the return of donated property which may have been claimed as a tax deduction. The natural history/anthropology policy does not allow the return of objects to donors, but does make an exception for NAGPRA and acknowledges that it is appropriate for the former owner to reacquire an object at public auction.

The other policies do allow the return of objects to the donor. Three policies (general, history, and natural history/anthropology) use an "if all else fails" approach. If no other means of disposal are available, return to the donor is acceptable.

One history policy merely states, "where appropriate" the object may be returned to the donor. Another history museum has a policy that authorizes the museum to notify the original donors and give them the opportunity to regain ownership of the object: "If the donor chooses not to regain ownership, they will be notified as to its method of disposition."

An art museum policy states: "On occasion, a donor may wish to buy back an object given earlier. Such a transaction is discouraged, but may proceed with full disclosure according to stated deaccessioning policy and procedure."

8. Other

Two art policies mention the possibility of returning a deaccessioned object to the vendor; one mentions "for reimbursement." Another art policy suggests that a deaccessioned object may be disposed of "by some other means" if it is determined that the other means would yield no less than a public auction. A natural history/anthropology museum commented that material which, after reasonable effort, cannot be disposed of otherwise, may be turned over to surplus property.

Finally, there is the general museum policy which states that items of nominal value can be placed with the museum council for its fund raiser.

DISPOSITION OF FORGERIES/REPRODUCTIONS
        8 policies: 10 %
        6 Art
        1 History
        1 General

The policies that discuss forgeries are very much in agreement that forgeries are to be marked indelibly as such and never returned to the market without full disclosure. One art museum states that a forgery is not to be returned to the market, but instead should be returned to the source from which the museum acquired it. Reproductions are also to be marked indelibly and sold with full documentation.

ETHICS OF DISPOSITION

When discussing who is eligible to acquire a deaccessioned object, a number of museums refer to, or cite directly, the guidelines provided by the Association of Art Museum Directors in its publication, *Professional Practices in Art Museums* (1992): "No member of a museum's Board of Trustees, governing body, staff, or those whose association with the institution might give them advantage in acquiring the work, shall be permitted to acquire directly or indirectly a work deaccessioned by the museum, or otherwise to benefit from its sale or trade."

Throughout the deaccessioning policies, various museums define a number of relationships to the museum that they consider apply here: current employees, ex-employees, board members, trustees, officers, volunteers, family members of any of the preceding groups, representatives of any of the preceding groups. One public museum included city officials and a county museum included county officials and elected officials. A university museum mentioned that university faculty and students were to refrain from acquiring deaccessioned objects as well.

There were 46 policies (58 percent of the total submitted) that discussed the responsibilities of staff members, and others who have relationships with the museum, toward deaccessioned objects. Of these polices, the following breakdown occurred.

    38 policies: 48 %
    13 Art . . . . 34 %
    10 Natural History/Anthropology . . . . . 26 %
    8 History. . . . . 21 %
    7 General . . . . 18 %

These 38 policies direct that staff and other people affiliated with the museum are not to acquire deaccessioned objects. Most of the policies instruct that deaccessioned objects are not to be acquired under any circumstances, with one art museum stating that the intent is to avoid a conflict of interest or even the appearance of it. Another general museum, in directing that deaccessioned objects not be acquired, says, "the museum cannot afford to be recognized as an institution which sells or gives away its collections."

Two policies (general and art) state that the people affiliated with the museum are not to acquire deaccessioned material, even at public auction and several other policies use wording from the AAMD policy that states that items are not to be acquired either "directly or indirectly." However, 10 of these policies (three history, three natural history/anthropology, three general, one art) use the wording: "objects will not be given or sold privately" to museum affiliates. While not stating that acquiring objects at public auction is acceptable, the wording seems to indicate that public auctions are a possible means of acquiring an object while remaining within the confines of the museum's policy.

    8 policies: 10%
    3 History
    2 Art
    2 Natural History/Anthropology
    1 General

These eight policies specifically mention that there are some circumstances where it is acceptable for people affiliated with the museum to acquire a deaccessioned object. Most of the policies stated that the only acceptable means of acquiring a deaccessioned object is when objects are sold at public auction or otherwise clearly offered for sale in a public marketplace.

One history policy states that "no officer or member of the society, or employee of the [museum] shall receive such items except by a process which insures that no unfair advantage was gained through their office."

IV. Use of Proceeds

In the policies that discuss the use of the proceeds from the sale of an object, a number of policies refer to the guidelines in the AAMD *Professional Practices in Art Museums* (1992): "Deaccessioning and disposal by sale shall not serve to provide operating funds, and the proceeds from disposal must be treated as acquisition funds."

There are also references to or wording that is similar to the guidelines issued by the AAM in its *Code of Ethics for Museums* (1993): "Disposal of collections through sale, trade or research activities is solely for the advancement of the museum's mission. Proceeds from the sale of nonliving collections are to be used consistent with the established standards of the museums discipline, but in no event shall they be used for anything other than acquisition or direct care of collections."

    59 policies: 75%
    21 Art 36%
    16 History 27%
    11 Natural History/Anthropology 19%
    11 General 19%

These 59 policies discuss how proceeds from sales of deaccessioned objects are to be used. Not all policies mention "use of proceeds." A number of museums direct that objects only be disposed by means of transfer to or exchange with another institution and, thus, have no proceeds to administer.

The 59 policies that discuss the use of proceeds break down along the following lines:

1. Policies that state that funds are to be used only for acquisitions
      35 policies: 59 % (of 59 policies)
         15 Art. . . . . 43 %
         8 Natural History/Anthropology . . . . . . 23 %
         7 History. . . . . 20 %
         5 General . . . . 14 %

The policies that instruct that funds be used only for acquisition are generally very straightforward in their wording, directing that funds be used for acquisitions only and, often, directing that funds be used in the same field or general category as the deaccessioned object. Two art policies direct that an effort should be made to acquire an object in the original donor's area of interest if it is possible to do so. One art policy comments that costs of selling an object may be deducted from the proceeds of a sale while another art policy states that expenses incurred in the disposal of an object will come from the museum's operations budget and are not be deducted from the proceeds of a sale. Four policies (two art, two history) specifically state that proceeds are not to be used as operating funds or to be used to subsidize the operation of the museum.

2. Policies that allocate funds to acquisition and conservation
      13 policies: 22 %
         5 History. . . . . 38 %
         4 Art. . . . . 31 %
         2 Natural History/Anthropology . . . . . . 15 %
         2 General . . . . 15 %

Policies that use funds for anything other than acquisitions usually direct that the funds only be used for conservation or care of collections purposes, using phrases like, "care and maintenance of collections" (natural history/anthropology), "collection purchases and/or conservation" (history), "exclusively for acquisition and conservation" (two art).

3. Other
>   11 policies: 19 %
>   4 History. . . . . 36 %
>   4 General . . . . 36 %
>   2 Art. . . . . 18 %
>   1 Natural History/Anthropology . . . . 9 %

A general policy states that funds are to be used for the purchase of new objects or direct care of objects in the collection but also notes "the meaning of 'direct care' has yet to be defined by the AAM. Until clear guidelines have been established, the museum will interpret this provision to the best of its ability and to the best of its understanding of the intent of the code and the best interests of the collection."

Two policies (general and history) state that proceeds be allocated toward acquisitions and/or for the "management" and preservation of the other items in the permanent collections. A history policy directs that proceeds be used for purchase of new acquisitions, the conservation of collection objects or the "improvement of collection storage facilities." A general policy directs that proceeds can be for "the purchase of objects and/or capital improvements designed to upgrade collections care." Two policies (history and natural history/anthropology) state that proceeds "will be used for enhancement of the collections," and an art policy states that proceeds are to be used to acquire other art objects or "to achieve other collection interests of the [museum]."

Finally, a college art policy states that "in the absence of grave financial exigency affecting the well-being of the college as a whole . . . funds realized from the disposal of objects will be credited to [the museum's] acquisitions fund."

CONCLUSION

It is clear that many museums are thinking carefully about their deaccessioning procedures and policies, but it should be noted that the policies submitted vary across a broad range, from detailed policies that consider many or most of the elements in the preceding review, to policies that are one page in length and provide only minimal guidance to staff members attempting to undertake a potentially very risky task for their institution. Because deaccessioning can, on occasion, lead to very negative press and public criticism, any museum that deaccessions objects needs to review its deaccessioning policies and make sure that they provide the kind of instruction the professional staff and the governing boards of the institution need to follow in order to carry out deaccessioning properly and ensure that public trust is preserved.

Many of the policies reviewed are vague on issues concerning the establishment of clear title, abandoned property, and what is required in the event of a theft. Few policies address issues of ownership, especially when the object may potentially be claimed by another party (other than through NAGPRA legislation), hardly surprising given the complications that can arise, but it is an area that could use some development.

It is worth noting again those areas where there were some divergence of opinion in the policies. The handling of gifts for resale evoked a few opposing responses. The sale of objects through the museum shop also prompted different interpretations in a number of policies. It is particularly important that the shop not be perceived as an avenue by which the museum disposes of objects and any sale of an object that was once in the collection or even perceived to be in any way collection-related may be a bad precedent to set.

Another area where there were varying opinions was in policies that discussed whether an object should be returned to the original donor. It is worth considering whether the institution wishes to set a precedent that allows donors to think it is possible to retrieve objects once they have been given to the museum, and for many public institutions issues of ethics and legality must be considered before any action is taken.

When writing or reviewing a deaccession policy, one should look for imprecise language that is open to interpretation and possible misinterpretation. Use straightforward language that is clear and understandable. The phrase "doubtful potential for utilization in the foreseeable future," for example, seems to indicate a lack of conviction on the part of an institution looking for a reason to deaccession an object.

Finally, it is very encouraging to see how many institutions consider the needs of other institutions when deaccessioning. Many institutions, when discussing the manner of disposition of the object, make it a point to provide other institutions with an opportunity to acquire objects and make an effort to keep cultural and historic objects in the context in which they were originally created or used. Deaccessioning is done for many reasons and the goal of raising funds for new acquisitions is a worthy one, but consideration of the needs of other institutions, especially when deaccessioned objects can fulfill their original promise in a new educational setting, is laudable.

Many thanks to Noreen Ong Choe, assistant registrar of the Stanford University Museum of Art, who did a great deal of the early work gathering examples of deaccessioning policies. Thanks also to Pamela Watson, head registrar at the Detroit Institute of Arts, who also gathered deaccessioning policies and who added many cogent and thoughtful comments.

CONTRIBUTING INSTITUTIONS

	ART	HISTORY	NATURAL HISTORY/ ANTHROPOLOGY	GENERAL	TOTALS
	29 (38%)	22 (28%)	16 (20%)	12 (15%)	79
REGION					
Mid-Atlantic	0	2	0	2	4 (5%)
Midwest	6	3	2	1	12 (15%)
Mountain Plains	0	3	1	0	4 (5%)
New England	5	1	0	1	7 (9%)
South	1	1	0	1	3 (4%)
West	16	12	13	8	49 (62%)
STAFF SIZE					
1-5	3	10	5	1	19 (24%)
6-25	12	6	5	7	30 (38%)
26-50	6	1	1	0	8 (10%)
51-100	2	1	1	1	5 (6%)
101-150	0	1	0	0	1 (1%)
151+	4	1	3	1	9 (11%)
Unknown	1	2	1	3	7 (9%)
GOVERNING CONTROL					
Federal	0	1	0	1	2 (3%)
State	0	3	2	2	7 (9%)
Municipal	1	2	2	3	8 (10%)
County	2	3	0	3	8 (10%)
Society	0	5	0	0	5 (6%)
Nonprofit	14	7	7	3	31 (39%)
University	11	0	5	1	17 (22%)
Unknown	0	1	0	0	1 (1%)

Index